M000282561

FUNDAMENTALS OF QUALITATIVE RESEARCH

This book is the road map to proficiency and development in the field of qualitative research. Borrowing from a wealth of experience teaching introductory qualitative research courses, author Kakali Bhattacharya lays out a dynamic program for learning different paradigms of inquiry, empowering students to recognize the convergence of popular research methodologies as well as the nuances and complexities that set each of them apart. Her book:

- supplements the readings and activities in a qualitative methods class, exposing students to the research process and the dominant types of qualitative research;
- introduces a variety of theoretical perspectives in qualitative research, including positivism and postpositivism, interpretivism, feminism, symbolic interactionism, phenomenology, hermeneutics, critical theory, and Critical Race Theory;
- identifies and summarizes the three dominant methodological approaches in qualitative research: narrative inquiry, grounded theory, and ethnography;
- provides interactive activities and exercises to help students crystallize their understanding of the different topics in each chapter.

Kakali Bhattacharya, Ph.D., is an associate professor in the Department of Educational Leadership at Kansas State University.

FUNDAMENTALS OF QUALITATIVE RESEARCH

A Practical Guide

Kakali Bhattacharya

Routledge
Taylor & Francis Group

NEW YORK AND LONDON

First published 2017
by Routledge
711 Third Avenue, New York, NY 10017

and by Routledge
2 Park Square, Milton Park, Abingdon, Oxon, OX14 4RN

Routledge is an imprint of the Taylor & Francis Group, an informa business

© 2017 Taylor & Francis

Library of Congress Cataloging-in-Publication Data
Names: Bhattacharya, Kakali, author.
Title: Fundamentals of qualitative research : a practical guide /
    by Kakali Bhattacharya.
Description: New York : Routledge, 2017. | Includes bibliographical
    references and index.
Identifiers: LCCN 2016037018 | ISBN 9781611321326 (hardback) |
    ISBN 9781611321333 (pbk.) | ISBN 9781611321340 (ebk.)
Subjects: LCSH: Qualitative research.
Classification: LCC H62 .B478 2017 | DDC 001.4/22—dc23
LC record available at https://lccn.loc.gov/2016037018

ISBN: 978-1-61132-132-6 (hbk)
ISBN: 978-1-61132-133-3 (pbk)
ISBN: 978-1-315-23174-7 (ebk)

Typeset in Bembo
by Apex CoVantage, LLC

Printed in Canada

To my Maa
Sumita

Who to this day does not exactly know what I do
With this thing called qualitative research
But she shares with anyone who would care to listen
That she is proud of me.
I dedicate this book to her open-hearted love.

CONTENTS

ACKNOWLEDGMENTS

This book has taken years in its making. What started out as handouts in my qualitative methods classes culminated in this book, and for that I need to thank several people. To Norman Denzin, thank you for introducing me to Mitch Allen, who placed enormous faith in me, when I was this new academic, fresh out of graduate school. This book was Mitch's vision, for which he gave me countless rounds of feedback. My deep gratitude to Mitch for never giving up on this book or me. To my students in my qualitative research classes who offered loving, critical feedback that continued to shape the book over the years – this book is as much theirs as it is mine. To Beverly Cross, for taking a chance on me early on and piloting this book in her classes and offering me feedback – I thank you for dissolving academic hierarchies to support this project. Special thanks to Jeong-Hee Kim for helping me realize that this book had become more than a "workbook" and suggesting its current title. Thank you Jeong-Hee for your countless hours of listening to me and offering me advice whenever I felt stuck or frustrated in the writing process.

To my mentors at the University of Georgia, without whom I would have never imagined a career of being a qualitative methodologist – there are just not enough words through which I can express my gratitude. Kathleen deMarrais, Kathy Roulston, and Jude Preissle have modeled the kind of mentoring that humbles me. To this day they stand with me, well over a decade after graduation; they offer me advice, think with me on various qualitative research issues, and inspire me to be a methodologist who helps people conceptualize and execute qualitative research situated in multiple paradigms, and not just the one in which I love to play.

To Hannah Shakespeare, Hannah Slater, and others at Routledge – thank you for working with me at the terminal stages of this project, when so much was already done as this work passed from Left Coast Press to you. Your guidance, patience, flexibility, and willingness to work with me have inspired me to develop a long-term relationship with Routledge. I remain deeply grateful for the countless hours you have already invested in this project with me.

To my partner Paul Maxfield and my dog Gigi Bhattacharya Maxfield the first™ – thank you Paul for being patient with me as I wrote this book. Thank you for listening to me talk about this book and its contents ad nauseam for years now. Thank you for feeding me and taking care of the house while I wrote this book. Thank you Gigi for being the best arm-rest, pillow, stress buster, and nap companion anyone could ever ask for. You are both the light of my life.

Finally, I extend my deepest gratitude to my mother. An academic herself, her relentless enthusiasm for learning is contagious. The amount of tenacity and perseverance she has demonstrated for surviving against all odds has been awe-inspiring. Years ago at a qualitative conference, a senior, well-known scholar dismissed this work by saying, "Oh this is just about teaching qualitative methods." Having seen my mother teaching in classrooms, connecting with people across age, culture, and other axes of difference, I can say now with confidence that to be able to communicate one's knowledge to a wide interdisciplinary audience has been one of the hardest things I have ever had to do. So to my mother, I dedicate this book, because it is her passion for teaching, creating entry points for learners, and arousing curiosity and wonder about inquiry that became the foundation of this book.

USING THIS BOOK

This handbook is designed as a supplementary text for any introductory qualitative methods class. Generally speaking, this book is not intended to be a standalone textbook; however, students can use this book as a refresher and can return to it for a quick reference.

What started out as handouts in class has culminated in this book. Every week as I would teach my introductory qualitative methods class, I would create handouts to bridge between some of the dense readings and assignments. I have been using Michael Crotty's (1998) text *The Foundations of Social Research: Meaning and Perspective in the Research Process* in my classes. Students sometimes found the readings to be a bit too dense for their liking, but I have felt strongly about introducing students to some of the history of social science and a well-synthesized narrative about the development of various theoretical and methodological perspectives that inform social science research. Thus, I began to create some handouts, make interactive activities, and list additional resources, etc. Eventually these handouts, activities, and resources for each week became a unit, as seen in this book. The units are arranged topically for each week with exercises peppered in as relevant.

What I found in my introductory qualitative methods classes is that when students meet qualitative methods for the first time, they struggle not only with learning a different paradigm of inquiry, but also with translating and internalizing some of the abstract concepts. This book allows for connecting concepts in various qualitative methods textbooks with experiential learning.

I have used this book with various texts that I have tried in my introductory qualitative research methods classes. Students have been able to follow along no matter what textbook I have switched to in different semesters. Most importantly, this book makes qualitative research accessible to different types of learners and mitigates some of the anxiety students have when they meet qualitative research for the first time. I intend for this book to be useful anywhere in the world, helping students learn qualitative inquiry in a way that does not oversimplify the discipline and yet preserves some of the complexity and nuances.

Golden Nuggets

At the end of each unit I have added a golden nugget. This golden nugget is a concluding reflective interactive activity that often pulls together the concepts of the unit. Readers can use the activity to assess their understanding of the unit and identify gaps in their understanding. Additionally, readers can use the activity included under golden nuggets to crystallize their understanding. Usually in class I assign a few minutes at the end to do some reflective exercises where students identify an idea that resonated, or something with which they were in conflict, or something that they need to think about some more, or an idea that crystallized their understanding of a topic. The golden nuggets offered in this book are my attempt to demonstrate the spirit of reflection as we conclude a unit.

1

UNIT 1: MEETING QUALITATIVE METHODS

So you are new to qualitative methods and do not really know what it is and how to think about it. To top it off, you have to understand the methods, the dense theories, the new language and terms, but also do projects and maybe even some data analysis. Sure, sounds overwhelming to me. This book is designed to help you:

- supplement the readings and activities in a qualitative methods class
- have a space to explore your understanding of qualitative research
- use it as a reference manual for your qualitative projects.

Intentions of This Unit

In this unit, learners will be introduced to the ways in which ideas about reality and truth are taken up in research. Additionally, they will be exposed to the elements of an empirical study, the research process, and the ways to identify these elements in existing qualitative research articles.

Truth, Reality, and Meaning in Research

How one understands truth and reality has a direct bearing on the kind of research one conducts. One way of understanding the concepts of truth, reality, and meaning is to situate them outside of conscious processing. In other words, a chair remains a chair, regardless of whether someone identifies a chair as such. This way of understanding a chair means that there are some inherent stable characteristics of a chair that exist regardless of whether an observer perceives those characteristics. Understanding truth, reality, and meaning this way is not right or wrong, but an approach some people take when thinking about research, and informing their research purpose, their questions, and the way they want to design and report their research. Researchers operating from this understanding of truth, reality, and meaning aim to capture truth that can exist as truth, regardless of who views it, who processes it, and who derives meaning from it. This would be considered to be objectivist truth. The assumption in this kind of knowledge making is that with appropriate processes, verifiable information can be recorded and reported objectively, and repeatedly with similar results, thus generating predictability and generalizability. Chances are, you are probably well familiar with this type of understanding of research.

Another way of understanding the concepts of truth, reality, and meaning is to situate these ideas within the perceptions of the observer and argue that these ideas only take shape within the human consciousness. A chair is not a chair until it is perceived to be so through a human mind and that nothing exists without being processed by human consciousness. In this way of thinking about truth and reality, meaning is constructed based on people's own understanding of their worlds, experiences, interaction with events, and circumstances in their lives. These kinds of truths, realities, and meanings are relative, situated, and context-driven.

There are other variations of truth and meaning making known as subjectivism and pragmatism, which are not discussed in this book. A decent discussion of these approaches can be found in Michael Crotty's book titled *The Foundations of Social Research: Meaning and Perspective in the Research Process*.

Objectivist and Constructivist Ways of Knowing

Remember, objectivist ways of knowing promote knowing that relies on stable characteristics of the object that can be verified regardless of who the observer is. In other words, a tree would be a tree regardless of whether there is someone to observe the tree being a tree. Constructivist ways of knowing would purport the tree is only a tree when an observer constructs meaning about the object with the characteristics of a tree.

Shifting Between Knowing: Interactive Exercise

Complete the following table with your understanding of objectivist and constructivist perspectives.

TABLE 1.1 Examples of Objectivist and Constructivist Ways of Knowing

	Objectivist	*Constructivist*
Heart	A muscular organ, which is hollow, that pumps blood through the circulatory system through dilation and contraction.	A place from where one feels love for other human beings.
Table	A piece of furniture with flat horizontal surface supported by four legs.	A place where one can dance in a bar with adequate amount of alcohol intake.
Dog?		
Your research topic?		

Instructor Note: If students struggle to think about their research topic from an objectivist perspective, guide them to think about the topic in closed-ended ways, where there is a yes/no answer or questions about causes or effects are being asked, or questions about differences are being asked. In other words, questions that take the format of "Is there a difference between X and Y?" or "Does X cause Y?" could start the thinking process on objectivist ways of knowing. If they still struggle, it might be an opportunity to discuss the probable nature of social science research and how absolute, 100 percent objective, and generalizable claims in social science research are nonexistent.

The Black Box of Research: Interactive Exercise

This is a class exercise I have conducted to help students understand the various ways in which meaning making occurs. This exercise works if the materials used in the exercise are kept hidden from the students. Students, if you want to do this exercise on your own, then have someone else create a box for you so you do not know what is inside the box.

- Take an empty box and put various objects inside it. These could be objects such as paperclips, pencils, stones, or paper. Or it could be objects like a small piece of sponge, a comb, or a glowing ball. Seal the box so that no content can come out of the box or can be seen.
- Repeat this process with several boxes, enough where a group of three to four students can work with one box.
- Ask students to document what they would consider to be objectivist truths and constructionist truths about the contents in the box. What would be something that could be agreeable across multiple groups of people in terms of statements made about the contents inside the box? What could be agreeable about the contents of the box if only two people share the same perception? Could there be items in the box that are not knowable, or not knowable fully?
- Connect the claims made by students to the nature of inquiry in social sciences. What is measurable? What is knowable? How much can truly be known if at all? What can be said about what is not knowable in tangible terms but still influences some form of meaning making?
- At the end of the exercise, please do not open the box. Students often want to know exactly what is inside the box. This is where we get into the discussion about research where nothing is ever 100 percent knowable, generalizable, predictable, or holistic—that we can come as close as we possibly can, but our claims are never fully absolute and we use many probabilistic and tentative tools to construct knowledge from research.

After conducting the activity, students should reflect on the following in their research journals. Students, if you do not have a research journal, then start one, where you would document your thoughts about everything that comes up during your academic journey.

What ways do you understand the process of inquiry now? When determining what was inside the boxes, what did you use as your criteria? What did you miss? How did you compare to other people in your group? What does this tell you about your approach to inquiry?

Elements of Research

Before any discussion of qualitative research, it is important to focus on what counts as research. Michael Crotty describes research as having four elements. These elements are methods, methodology, theoretical perspective, and epistemology. Throughout this book, I will be referring to these terms in various levels of detail. **Methods** refer to the ways in which data collection occurs in research. These could include interviews, observations, surveys, etc. **Methodology** is akin to the blueprint of the research study. It is the design of the study, the master plan for executing all aspects of the study. **Theoretical perspective** is the lens through which we try to understand our studies. This lens offers us some way to organize our thoughts, lay out our assumptions and beliefs, and logically defend the organizing patterns through which we might want to explore the topic of our interest. And **epistemology** is basically the way we know our world. I would also add to it another concept, **ontology**, which refers to our nature of being. Later in this unit, I will elaborate more on these ideas and how they specifically inform the research process. When all these elements are aligned, you can argue that you have a rigorous study.

Quantitative research aims to discover certain patterns that can be captured and predicted accurately with some degree of confidence that something beyond coincidence is occurring which is generalizable to a population of interest. Qualitative research, on the other hand, aims to work within the context of human experiences and the ways in which meaning is made out of those experiences. Qualitative researchers take different approaches when constructing knowledge about human experiences. The theoretical perspective held by a qualitative researcher plays a key role in informing what a qualitative study might look like. This idea will be elaborated further in this unit.

Searching for Research: Interactive Exercise

Using your library databases, find at least three peer-reviewed empirical studies that were conducted using qualitative methods. Keep these three articles handy as we will be referring to these articles throughout the handbook. Look through these articles and answer the following questions:

What were the research purposes listed in the articles? What did you notice about how the research purposes were framed?

What, if any, were the research questions listed in the articles?

What were the reasons given, if any, for conducting this study using qualitative inquiry?

What stood out to you about qualitative research as you read through the papers? Which parts appeared to be new or different knowledge for you?

Qualitative Research and Culture

Qualitative research has had early roots in anthropology and sociology. Researchers from the Western world would visit exotic cultures and study people and their customs and rituals through interviews, observations, and archived materials. Then the researcher would try to put together an in-depth cultural description, usually known as ethnography, which highlighted common patterns that existed across data sources. Thus, people who did not visit that specific part of the world would get an understanding of a different culture through the research of anthropologists and sociologists. Margaret Mead (Bateson & Mead, 1942) and James Clifford (Clifford, 1994) are some of the famous scholars associated with ethnography.

This way of thinking about culture limited the understanding of culture to customs and behavior of people who were non-White, who became the object of the researcher's gaze, who most often was White. Being cultural outsiders meant that any knowledge constructed about another group of people reflected the researcher's background and understanding of what it meant to be civilized, backwards, normal, different, etc. In other words, the researcher's epistemology was connected to the construction of knowledge of another group of people.

This model of qualitative research has come under attack from various groups such as "Third World" scholars, feminists, scholars of color, etc. These scholars question the notion of telling stories about someone else's culture from a Western perspective. They claim that someone who is trained in Western philosophies and science cannot possibly see the world in the ways of people who might not have been exposed or trained in the same philosophies. Margaret Mead was criticized for imposing her progressive upbringing on Samoan women by calling them oppressed. Oppression and liberation look different to Samoan women than they do to Margaret Mead. Therefore, Mead's understanding of oppression cannot be the same reality as the Samoan women, whose stories she was trying to tell (Foerstel & Gilliam, 2009).

Decolonizing scholar Linda Tuhiwai Smith (1999/2012) documents the problems surrounding outsiders conducting research **on** indigenous people from the perspective of the Maori people in New Zealand. Her work details various unethical research practices, such as scalping and filling Maori people's skulls with millet seeds to deem them less than human based on how many seeds the skulls can contain. Evoking the history of being once colonized and researched, Smith's work provides cautionary tales for cultural outsiders.

To understand culture, we need to see culture as more than one's ethnic background. Culture should evoke ideas such as shared values, beliefs, rituals, language, and clothing, among other things that membership in a group could be associated with. Could you think of a culture in which you belong which is not just associated with your ethnic background? For example, when I think of a doctoral student culture, I think of the students who are reading and writing fiercely, attempting to complete coursework or working on a dissertation study, speaking in specific academic language, sleep deprived at certain times during the semester, dependent on caffeine, and carrying a book bag at all times.

What Is Your Culture? Interactive Exercise

Select a box, paper bag, or any kind of container to hold things. Then walk around your home and pick up anything that resembles who you are, what is meaningful to you, rituals in which you participate, your style, groups in which you belong, etc. There is no right or wrong way to do this. Once you have gathered all your objects, pull them out. Look at them carefully. Think of what the objects signify, perhaps a value, a belief, a membership in a group, a weekly or monthly or yearly ritual. Next, reflect on the following questions:

What values were you able to identify from your objects? What groups do you belong to that share the same values?

Thinking back on the objects, shared values and beliefs, and groups in which you belong, think of what makes you a member of the group. How does one become a member of the groups that share your similar values, beliefs, etc.?

Do these objects reflect a specific type of language use, some coded shared understanding with those that share the same values and beliefs with you?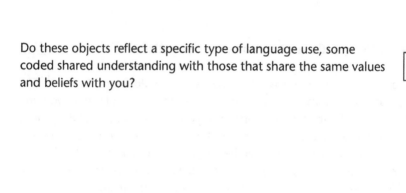

Reflecting on the objects and people who share similar values and beliefs, and might even be part of the same group with you, can you think of how an outsider can become an insider to these ideas, values, and beliefs?

How would you label the ways in which these objects point to your sense of belongingness with people who share similar ideas, beliefs, and values? Could you give yourselves a name for your cultural group?

Qualitative Research and the Research Process

To understand the structure of research, refer to my hourglass model of research in Figure 1.1. Before we discuss the hourglass model, it is critical to state that even though we are going to talk of the components of the model in a linear fashion, in reality the process of conducting qualitative research is nonlinear and iterative, with the researcher going back and forth across various components represented in the hourglass model.

Ontology refers to your nature of being. It might be hard to articulate or pinpoint what that is for you specifically if this is the first time you are hearing of this concept, but when you think about it, there are some things you know resonate well with your nature of being and others not. It is precisely that resonance that motivates you to your actions, and to your desire for the topic of your scholarly inquiry.

Epistemology focuses on how we know what we know. For qualitative inquiry, there is an understanding that people construct their own meanings based on their interactions with the world called **constructionism**. Thus constructionism is the epistemology that informs **MOST** qualitative research. However, there are other epistemologies such as subjectivism and pragmatism that can also inform

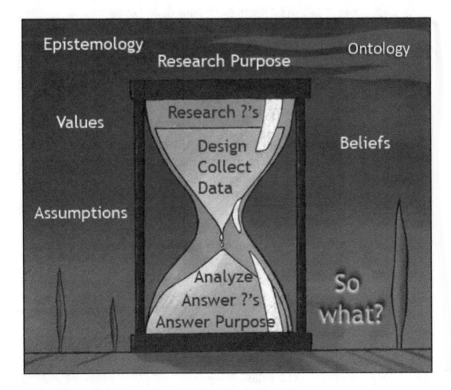

FIGURE 1.1   Bhattacharya Hourglass Model of Research

qualitative work. The selection of research purpose and questions is a direct reflection of your epistemology because you have made a cognitive choice for these specific research purpose and questions over many others.

Let us work with an example. A few years ago, I conducted a study where I wanted to explore how students in my qualitative research class experienced the use of wikis in the class to learn the content. Wikis are editable webpages that students could use to work collaboratively on a project. The study has now been published in an online journal titled *Technology, Humanities, Education and Narrative*. You can find the article here: http://thenjournal.org/feature/307/printable/. A data set for this study is included at the end of this book for your reference. This data set includes a sample interview, a researcher journal entry, a participant journal entry, and a sample wiki page.

My epistemological assumption was that students constructed meaning out of their experiences of using wiki while collaboratively working on a project with their peers. I assumed that an inquiry should be made to explore how these constructed meanings shaped students' learning experiences in my class. These ideas shaped the research purpose and questions.

The purpose of the research was to identify the ways in which wikis play a role in shaping the construction, negotiation, and contestation of knowledge in web-supported graduate-level classes. Particular research questions that guided the project were:

i)   In what ways do learners build a community of practice using wikis to construct knowledge?
ii) How do learners negotiate their own voices in relation to others' voices in wiki-based learning environments in graduate-level classes?
iii) What kinds of knowledge are constructed through the collaborative participation of learners and an instructor using wiki-based learning spaces?

Once you have identified your research purpose and research questions, you need to outline your research design. This is the blueprint for the research. The design could guide specifically the sources of data collection, the timeline of the research, the roles you want the participants to play, and all the ways in which you could collect data in your study. Additionally, the design could inform the kind of data analysis you wish to conduct for your research, informed by your epistemology, theoretical framework, and research purpose and questions. It is also important to note that no research design is complete without an awareness of theoretical perspectives and how those perspectives will play a role in the study. In a later section in this unit, we will discuss theoretical perspectives.

> If you look at the wiki article example, you will see various aspects of the research design laid out so that the reader can see how the research was conducted, what was collected as data, and for how long, including a raw data inventory table that lists 2206 pages of raw data collected. You will also see that theoretical perspectives are discussed in advance of research design.

After you have identified what you want to inquire, how you want to inform your inquiry, and what it might look like, you would mostly likely consider what would count as data for your study. While there are many discussions about what counts as data in qualitative research (Bogdan & Biklen, 2003; Charmaz, 2008; Richards, 2005; Ryan & Bernard, 2003), you will have to make some decisions about what you would like to include as data with an awareness that as you conduct your study, your understanding and inclusion of what might be sources of information could change. However, traditionally, qualitative researchers have used interviews, observations, artifacts, and anything else that adds to the understanding of the research topic.

Moreover, qualitative researchers also keep **a researcher journal** during data collection and analysis in order to record their thoughts, reactions, hunches, assumptions, and beliefs to analyze how they influence the data collection and analysis. It is not **wrong** to have values, as we all have them. In qualitative research, we claim them, own them, and document how these values shape our study. Keep in mind that not all qualitative studies have to include all data sources. You just have to defend your choice to use what you decide to be the sources of information that assist in answering your research purpose and questions.

Data analysis is another consideration you have to make in qualitative research which will inform your presentation of findings, discussion, conclusion, and implications. Notice in Figure 1.1 that you start the research process from a broad scope which narrows as you collect data and then broadens when you begin to answer research questions and purpose.

> In the wiki example, you will find a detailed explanation of the data management and data analysis process. Often this is the part that sometimes is least explained in articles or not well explained. Note that data analysis in qualitative research is a messy process, so the outcomes of these processes are often messy and unstable. In particular, if I begin with an epistemological assumption of constructionism, then I have an obligation to honor multiple ways of constructing meaning about the data.

Finally, when you have answered your research purpose, you need to claim the value of your research. You need to answer the big "So what?" question. What is your point? What are the implications of this research? How does your research matter within the context of the topic, discipline? This is the most difficult part of doing research because many people think that unless their research is earth-shattering, they cannot make any claims. I am going to tell you a secret that will help you tremendously in your academic careers: **You do not have to solve the whole world's problem with one research project, even if it is your dissertation!!!**

Identifying the Parts: Interactive Exercise

Remember the three peer-reviewed articles you looked at earlier th
were driven by qualitative inquiry? Refer back to those three articl
how much of the following table you can complete based on your understanding of the material covered thus far in this unit. What are you able to
identify? What are you struggling with? Use your researcher journal (paper-
based or digital) to start documenting your thoughts about what you read.

TABLE 1.2 Identifying Scholarly Elements in a Research Article

	Article 1	*Article 2*	*Article 3*
Theoretical framework			
Research design			
Data collection methods			
Findings			
Implications			

Remember, you are not obligated to understand everything you read. Let the language and the ideas presented here wash over you. Let go of the anxiety that you did not "get" a certain part. Instead, focus on things that resonated with you, things that stood out to you.

Golden Nuggets: Interactive Exercise

As we conclude this chapter, reflect on the following prompts. Feel free to use your researcher journal if you need more space.

Five key ideas that have resonated with me from this chapter are:

One or two questions I have now about qualitative research are:

2

UNIT 2: TERRAIN AND TYPES OF QUALITATIVE RESEARCH

You are now familiar with the elements of a research process, the ways in which qualitative research is published in scholarly journals, and how those elements of the research process are embedded in scholarly work. In this unit you will be exposed to a deeper understanding of qualitative research, including the various purposes and types of qualitative research.

Intentions of This Unit

In this unit, learners will be exposed to the research process, the terrain of qualitative research, and the dominant types of qualitative research. This is not an exhaustive list of qualitative research, but just an introduction, with suggested additional readings.

Terrain of Qualitative Research

For a study to be rigorous there should be an alignment between epistemology, theoretical framework, methodology, methods, data analysis, representation, and implications. For quantitative research, criteria of reliability, validity, and generalizability are used for determining the "scientific" value of research. However, the same criteria for "scientific" are not applicable for qualitative research. Quantitative research usually attempts to predict a trend across a broad sample of people. Qualitative research conducts in-depth inquiries within a small sample of population. Figure 2.1 is a representation of qualitative and quantitative research.

Thus, quantitative and qualitative research are complementary with different purpose and focus. Using the criteria for quantitative research will not work for qualitative research because qualitative researchers usually work with interpreting people's stories, experiences, or specific discourses. While there are several ways

FIGURE 2.1   Schematic Representation of Quantitative and Qualitative Research

to describe the terrain of qualitative research, the organization of the terrain that I have found most useful is Patti Lather's (1991) work in *Getting Smart: Feminist Research and Pedagogy With/in the Postmodern.* There, she outlines three broad purposes of qualitative research, which do not include the need to predict or generalize. Instead, qualitative researchers conduct studies to:

- understand
- interrogate
- deconstruct

If a qualitative researcher is trying to **understand** someone's experiences, then s/he conducts a study where s/he collects all relevant information surrounding the experience and reports them. The goal is to simply understand and explore in an in-depth manner and not to generalize. For example, I might be interested in exploring the experiences of African American women, who are graduate students in the College of Education at a predominantly White university. I know I cannot generalize and I do not want to. I want to do this research because I think that the stories that these women have to tell have not been heard or documented in academic spaces or perhaps needs more documentation. These stories are part of the history of education that are currently undocumented or poorly documented.

If the purpose of a qualitative study is to **interrogate**, then the researcher is assuming that the experiences people have are based on their gender, age, race, sexuality, and other forms of identification with various social categories. Such studies are usually conducted to highlight issues of inequities and marginalization, often with ideas for solution. Many forms of social justice research (Fine, 1991; Ladson-Billings, 1998) are conducted with the purpose to interrogate and identify workable solutions. Policy decisions are impacted by such studies. Work in the area of feminism, Critical Race Theory, and Marxism focus on the need to interrogate some kind of social structure that produces experiences of inequalities (Kaplan & Grewal, 1999; Ladson-Billings & Tate, 1995).

Finally, if the purpose of the qualitative research is to **deconstruct**, then researchers try to break apart assumptions, stereotypes, like Lego™ pieces. They see every social structure that produces experience of inequity to be breakable. The researcher assumes that people are socially conditioned to believe and see the

TABLE 2.1 Paradigms and Purpose of Qualitative Inquiry

Understand	Interrogate	Deconstruct
Interpretivism	Feminism	Postcolonial
Narrative Inquiry	Marxism	Poststructural
Phenomenology	Critical Theory	Diaspora

Based on: Lather (1991). *Getting smart: Feminist research and pedagogy with/in the postmodern.* New York: Routledge.

world a certain way. If the researcher can show the assumptions that maintain and replicate social conditioning, then s/he can break apart a structure. Imagine when you see a boat built with Lego™ pieces, you know that they are individual pieces of plastic that resemble the structure of a boat that can be broken apart to build another structure, perhaps a castle. You know that each structure is breakable and there are multiple possibilities to what you can create. Similarly, a deconstructivist sees the world in terms of structures that are built on smaller pieces of assumptions. If you break apart the assumptions, you break apart the structure. When the structure is broken, then people have the choice to create new structures any way they please. Because all structures can be breakable, deconstructivists do not provide fixed solutions to a problem. They expose the problem, break it apart, and let people come up with their own possibilities of structures. A deconstructivist knows that every structure has its limits and possibilities. Table 2.1 contextualizes the purpose and theoretical paradigms of qualitative research.

Please know that this table is just a loosely structured guideline for organizing various types of qualitative research. However, often researchers blur the boundary between the columns presented in Table 2.1 and even extend further. Nevertheless, for people meeting qualitative research for the first time, this table offers an initial framework to understand numerous types of qualitative inquiry.

The wiki example discussed earlier was an interpretive study. If you look at the article again (http://thenjournal.org/feature/307/printable/), you will find that there is a section within the article that discusses interpretivism as its framework. This is because the purpose of the study was to explore, understand, and describe. I was not setting up an inquiry to interrogate or break apart social structures.

Columns and Boundaries: Interactive Exercise

Using your library's databases, search for two qualitative research journals: *Qualitative Inquiry* and *International Journal of Qualitative Studies in Education*. Within each journal, look for empirical studies that can fall under each of the columns in Table 2.1. You can use the words under the columns for closer alignment. In other words, you can use the word "deconstruct" to look for an article that would belong to the third column. After you have attempted to locate at least three articles, one belonging to a different column, fill in the blanks.

List the article titles and the columns in which they fall.

List the research purpose and questions for each of the articles.

What was the rationalization provided for the theoretical perspective of each of the articles?

What challenges did you experience when identifying the articles? Did they
fit in the columns well? Did you want to blur the boundaries? Could they fit
in multiple columns?

Instructor Note: If this exercise is conducted in class, then it could also
serve as fertile grounds for discussing subjectivities and how they inform
theoretical perspectives based on the ways in which the students classified
the articles belonging to the three columns.

Academic Rigor in Qualitative Research

Often as new learners of qualitative research, you might have questions about how such a subjective form of inquiry could be considered rigorous. You might even be in thesis or dissertation committees where a committee member could ask you such a question. The truth is that no matter how diligent, systematic, and organized you might be, once you present your study to the world, you cannot ensure that everyone reading your work will make the identical assessment of your work. Your work might be applauded by some and criticized by others. However, you can make some arguments as to the ways in which you attempted to conduct rigorous work, based on how you situated your understanding of "rigor" within your ontological, epistemic, theoretical, and methodological frameworks.

The following are some of the ways in which qualitative researchers have attempted to maintain rigor in their studies (note these ideas are driven by different theoretical perspectives, and therefore are not meant to be a checklist for all qualitative studies):

- The **alignment** of epistemology, theoretical frameworks, methodology, and methods, data analysis, and representation (see Figure 1.1)
- Acknowledging and documenting the **iterative** nature of qualitative research where the researcher often goes back and forth between various stages of research based on shifting epistemologies, data collection, data analysis, research ethics, and representation
- The integration and interrogation of information from **multiple data sources** as evidence
- The **prolonged duration** of data collection to develop an in-depth understanding
- The open discussion and interrogation of the researcher's **values, assumptions, and beliefs** and how they inform the study
- The justification of research design based on **literature review** in specific theoretical and methodological arenas
- The various types of checks conducted during the research:

  o   Member checks (checking with the participant repeatedly to ensure shared understanding of meanings)
  o   Peer debriefing (working with a peer who is informed with methodology and topic for academic rigor)
  o   Subjectivity interview (researcher allows a peer to interview her/him so that s/he can become aware of values, assumptions, and beliefs that inform the research)
  o   Reflective journaling before, during, and after the research

- Finding ways to **falsify/complicate/problematize** the researcher's own interpretation of data to develop an awareness for alternate perspectives that the researcher might not be able to address otherwise

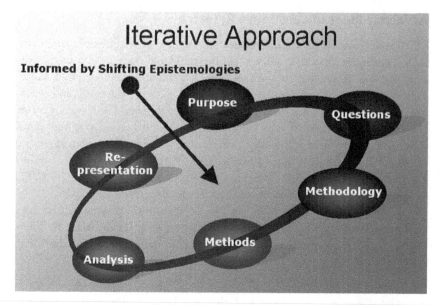

FIGURE 2.2 Iterative Approach and Alignment in Qualitative Research

- Identifying ways in which the research can be understood in terms **of multiple limits and possibilities** instead of presenting research as an absolute truth
- Presenting findings with **rich contextual details** so that a reader can have multiple entry points into the research
- **Anticipating and addressing criticism** of the research
- **Ethical** engagement in the research process, data analysis, data representation, and relationship with the participants
- **Substantive** and/or **methodological** contribution to existing literature.

Figure 2.2 demonstrates the basic structure of qualitative research that needs to be in alignment to make compelling arguments towards the academic rigor and trustworthiness of a study. However, this is not to say that researchers cannot come up with additional forms of documentation, reflections, checks, and alignments according to their own sensibilities and alignments with ontology, epistemology, methodology, and representation of data.

Common Types of Qualitative Studies

The following is a list of the common types of qualitative studies. This is not an exhaustive list, and there are as many possibilities of doing qualitative research as there are researchers. The descriptions are brief with seminal citations for you to explore on your own for more information.

Ethnography

Ethnography is the study of people within the context of their culture. Generally speaking, ethnography involves the researcher being immersed in the culture that she is studying and situating herself within the cultural context (otherwise known as the field) for a prolonged period of time, extending well beyond a year. The understanding of the culture or a group of people and their everyday activities generally, comes from documenting ongoing events, conducting interviews, and collecting archived materials where possible.

Some seminal pieces to learn more about ethnography are:

Lecompte, M.D., & Preissle, J. (1993). *Ethnography and qualitative research design in educational research*. San Diego, CA: Emerald Group Publishing.
Van Maanen, J. (1988). *Tales of the field: On writing ethnography*. Chicago, IL: The University of Chicago Press.
Wolcott, H.F. (2008). *Ethnography: A way of seeing*. Lanham, MD: Altamira Press.

Critical Ethnography

One of the key ideas that guides critical ethnographies is that any kind of social documentary of human lives is embedded in various power relations and inequities. Therefore, ethnographic tales cannot be told without including the ways in which power functions in those tales. Like many other forms of qualitative research, critical ethnography has many definitions and is taken up in various ways by social scientists. Therefore, the best way I approach critical ethnography is where a study of culture is conducted with the intent to interrogate some social structures which lead to experiences of inequity.

Some seminal pieces to learn more about critical ethnography are:

Carspecken, F.P. (1995). *Critical ethnography in educational research: A theoretical and practical guide (critical social thought)*. New York, NY: Routledge.
Madison, S.D. (2005). *Critical ethnography: Method, ethics, and performance*. Thousand Oaks, CA: Sage Publications.
Thomas, J. (1993). *Doing critical ethnography*. Thousand Oaks, CA: Sage Publications.

Autoethnography

This is a form of qualitative inquiry where the researcher takes a personal, reflexive journey into parts of her experiences and systematically analyzes those experiences within the cultural context of where those experiences occur. The reason one might want to conduct autoethnographic work could vary, but one of the reasons scholars conduct autoethnographic work is to document narratives that are otherwise absent in the mainstream research literature. Sometimes researchers use autoethnographic work for social justice causes where they use their experiences as grounds for deeper analysis of the effects of various social structures of oppression. Autoethnographic work is a combination of autobiography and ethnography.

Some seminal pieces to learn more about autoethnography are:

Ellis, C. (2004). *The ethnographic I: A methodological novel about autoethnography*. New York, NY: Altamira Press.

Ellis, C., & Bochner, A.P. (1996). *Composing ethnography: Alternative forms of qualitative writing*. Walnut Creek, CA: Altamira Press.

Jones, S.H., Adams, T., & Ellis, C. (Eds.). (2013). *Handbook of autoethnography*. San Francisco, CA: Left Coast Press.

Case Study

This type of research involves in-depth contextual study of a person, people, issue, and place, within a predetermined scope of the study. Usually highlighting the predetermined scope of a study is called bounding the study or creating a bounded system. This is done so that it is conceptually clear to both the researcher and the consumers of the research what the parameters of the study were, what the researcher was trying to study, and how the researcher drew boundaries around the gaze of his or her interest.

Some seminal pieces to learn more about case study are:

Merriam, S.B. (1998). *Qualitative research and case study applications in education*. San Francisco, CA: Jossey-Bass.

Stake, R.E. (1995). *The art of case study research*. Thousand Oaks, CA: Sage Publications.

Yin, R.K. (Ed.). (2003). *Case study research: Design and methods*. Thousand Oaks, CA: Sage Publications.

Interview Study

In this type of qualitative inquiry, interviews are the primary mode of inquiry, although other data sources are often used as additional data sources. There are various types of interview studies, such as in-depth interviews, open-ended interviews, critical incident interviews, feminist interviews, etc. Each of these types of interviews is driven by varied research purposes, research purposes, and theoretical perspectives of the researcher.

Some seminal pieces to learn more about interview study are:

deMarrais, K. (2004). Qualitative interview studies: Learning through experience. In K. deMarrais & S.D. Lapan (Eds.), *Foundations for research: Methods of inquiry in education and the social sciences* (pp. 51–68). Mahwah, NJ: Lawrence Erlbaum Associates.

Kvale, S., & Brinkmann, S. (2009). *InterViews: Learning the craft of qualitative research interviewing*. Thousand Oaks, CA: Sage Publications.

Spradley, J.P. (1979). *The ethnographic interview*. Belmont, CA: Wadsworth Group.

Narrative Inquiry

This type of qualitative study focuses on the story as the basic unit of analysis. In other words, researchers who use narrative inquiry are interested in understanding how people articulate their life experiences in the structure of a story. The structure of the story then becomes the points of analysis for a narrative inquiry–driven qualitative researcher.

Some seminal pieces to learn more about narrative inquiry are:

Clandinin, D.J. (Ed.). (2007). *Handbook of narrative inquiry: Mapping a methodology.* Thousand Oaks, CA: Sage Publications.
Polkinghorne, D.E. (1995). Narrative configuration in qualitative analysis. *International Journal of Qualitative Studies in Education, 8*(1), 5–23.
Kim, J.-H. (2015). *Understanding narrative inquiry: The crafting and analysis of stories as research.* Thousand Oaks, CA: Sage Publications.

Phenomenological Study

One of the most common types of qualitative studies conducted is phenomenological study. Phenomenological studies in qualitative research have deep philosophical roots that inform specific methodological procedures too. Phenomenological studies require participants to reflect on their experiences in as much detail as possible as part of experiencing a phenomenon. The purpose of this kind of study is to explore what a particular experience means for people who have experienced a shared phenomenon so that the structure of the experience can be understood and the essence of the experience can be abstracted.

Some seminal pieces to learn more about phenomenology are:

Elveton, R.O. (Ed.). (2003). *The phenomenology of Husserl: Selected critical readings.* Sydney, Australia: Noesis Press.
von Herrmann, F.-W. (2013). *Hermeneutics and reflection: Heidegger and Husserl on the concept of phenomenology.* Toronto, Canada: University of Toronto Press.
Manen, M.V. (2014). *Phenomenology of practice: Meaning-giving methods in phenomenological research and writing.* San Francisco, CA: Left Coast Press.

Grounded Theory

Grounded theory is another popular approach in qualitative research. This kind of qualitative inquiry offers some explicitly stated structure and sequence in the process of inquiry, which can be helpful to many researchers who are drawn to such structures. Researchers who use grounded theory usually develop a theory grounded in a deep, systematic, structured form of data analysis. However, there are strong differences of opinion in how one should approach this development of theory and the role the researcher plays in relationship with data. There are some arguments that the discovery process of the research should be conducted with as little interference of the researcher's prior experiences, or influence of prior theories. The proponents of this **objectivist** version of grounded theory expect the researcher to enter the research space with minimal predetermined ideas. This way the researcher would be able to bring some neutrality to the inquiry while recording events without having these events first filtered through preexisting hypotheses and biases.

However, **constructivist** grounded theorists advocate for recognizing that the researcher constructs her own meaning based on her interaction with the participant and various data sources, despite one's best attempt to not come to the research setting with predetermined ideas and theoretical influences. In essence grounded theory allows a researcher to have a systematic, structured approach, where the researcher is constantly comparing various pieces of data with each other to come to a place of saturation from where a theory can be discovered grounded in this extensive process of data analysis.

Some seminal pieces to learn more about grounded theory are:

Charmaz, K. (2006). *Constructing grounded theory: A practical guide through qualitative analysis.* Thousand Oaks, CA: Sage Publications.
Strauss, A., & Corbin, J. (1998). *Basics of qualitative research: Techniques and procedures for developing grounded theory* (2nd ed.). Thousand Oaks, CA: Sage Publications.

Oral History

This type of qualitative study focuses on telling the story of one person's life or of the lives of a group of people. The storytelling can be powerful based on the meanings made of the stories and the insights gained from bearing witness to those stories. Oral history projects could also be informed by a need to advocate for social justice issues. For example, oral history projects detailing stories from survivors of 9/11 and Hurricane Katrina tragedies in the United States of America could be immersed in various issues of inequity and how they played out in the lives of the storytellers. Oral history focuses on a story or a collection of stories from the life experiences of a person who can account for her firsthand knowledge of those experiences.

Some seminal pieces to learn more about oral history are:

Janesick, V. (2010). *Oral history for the qualitative researcher: Choreographing the story.* New York, NY: Guilford Press.
Leavy, P. (2011). *Oral history: Understanding qualitative research.* New York, NY: Oxford University Press.
Perks, R., & Thomson, A. (Eds.). (1998/2006). *The oral history reader.* New York, NY: Routledge.

Arts-Based Approaches to Qualitative Research

This approach to qualitative research has been continuously gaining momentum as qualitative researchers attempt to represent findings with complexity and multilayered sensibilities. Arts-based approaches to qualitative research propose adapting some tenets of the creative arts at various stages of qualitative research, especially leading to an artistic representation of findings in the end. Scholars who use this approach intersect the creative arts with qualitative research methods so that they could produce a dramatic, poetic, or some other form of artistic rendering of their work. For example, one could render a poetic representation from interviews, photo essays from collecting pictures during the study, or an ethnodrama that could integrate various data sources such as interviews, observations, and archived materials. The basic premise of arts-based approaches is to integrate scholarship, the creative arts, and research methodologies.

Some seminal pieces to learn more about arts-based approaches are:

Barone, T., & Eisner, E.W. (2012). *Arts-based research.* Thousand Oaks, CA: Sage Publications.
Knowles, J.G., & Cole, A.L. (2007). *Handbook of the arts in qualitative research: Perspectives, methodologies, examples, and issues.* Thousand Oaks, CA: Sage Publications.
Leavy, P. (2009/2015). *Method meets art: Arts-based research practice* (2nd ed.). New York, NY: Guilford Press.

Intersecting Ontology, Epistemology, and Methodology: Interactive Exercise

By now you have been introduced to various types of methodological approaches. It can become quite confusing to know what it is that you would like to choose for your area of interest. The following reflective activity could be of help.

1. On a piece of paper, draw (in any way you choose: doodle, crayons, paint, sketch) an interpretation of your values, beliefs, and assumptions, and a potential research interest (does not have to be fully formed yet). This could be done in any abstract form, as artistic skills are not necessary for this activity.
2. Draw a bridge or some other representation of connectivity from your values, beliefs, and assumptions to your research interest.
3. Are there any words or terms that can crystallize the connection between the various parts of your drawing?
4. Reflect on the following prompts. You can move back and forth from your drawing to the questions below because perhaps answering the questions might make you want to add more pieces to your drawing. I encourage you to not skip the drawing part as this is a process of inquiry in itself.

What is it that you want to know, if money, skills, knowledge were not an issue? What aspect of human behavior, human experience would you like to explore?

Why are you attracted to this topic? What is the appeal of this topic to you? Why does it matter?

Are you drawn to more linear and structured thinking, or are you drawn to messy, ambiguous, contradictory thoughts, or both? Explain and explore below.

Is the purpose of your research to understand, interrogate, or deconstruct?

Now take a look at the types of qualitative studies discussed earlier and identify one to three types of studies that speak to you. You are free to change your mind at any time.

As you complete the following section, reflect on the alignment and modify as necessary.

Your values, beliefs, assumptions:

Your potential research interest:

Your motivation, passion for this study:

A type of qualitative study that fits:

Your way of thinking (structured, messy, linear, contradictory):

Instructor Note: If this exercise is conducted in class, this can be a way to open up the connections between ontology, epistemology, theoretical perspectives, methodologies, and methods. I usually have the following table drawn out on the board to fill in with students' topics, and by the time the table is filled, students begin to notice the diversity of approaches and the ways in which various methods can be combined and recombined depending on the research topic, theoretical perspectives, and methodology.

Student Note: Students, you could also document your interests in the table below either here or in your journal. This will allow you to create a visual documentation of your research interests and how you are aligning yourself with theoretical and methodological approaches.

TABLE 2.2 Aligning Scholarly Elements in a Study

Research Topic	Theoretical Perspective(s)	Methodologies	Methods

By now, you should have a sense of your research interest and how it con-nects to your values, beliefs, and assumptions. You should also be able to identify a type of qualitative study that fits your way of thinking.

Golden Nuggets: Interactive Exercise

As we conclude this unit, use your research journal for the following activity.

1. Draw a mountain and a valley or a series of mountain and a valley.
2. On the peak of the mountain, list ideas that you have encountered in qualitative research that have risen to the surface and crystallized for you.
3. In the valley parts, list ideas that are still too dense, too foggy, that you are struggling with. You can do this activity in silence or with your favorite calming music in the background if it appeals to you.
4. In your journal, write about the ideas that you listed on the peaks and valleys. What resonated with you and why? What do you need to do to obtain clarity for the ideas listed in the peak? What makes those ideas especially challenging? How do your beliefs, assumptions, values align with the ideas you have listed in peaks and valleys?

3

UNIT 3: CONCEPTUALIZING QUALITATIVE RESEARCH

You have been exposed to the terrain of qualitative research and you have started applying these ideas to discover a research interest that could be explored through qualitative inquiry. In this unit, we will learn more about subjectivities and the structure of the qualitative research.

Intentions of This Unit

In this unit, learners will be introduced to the notion of subjectivities and the role subjectivities play in one's qualitative study. Learners will also be exposed to a general structure of dissertation informed by qualitative inquiry in the U.S.

Subjectivities

One article that I have recommended that students read early on in their exploration of qualitative research is Peshkin's (1988) article titled "In Search of Subjectivity: One's Own." Subjectivity has been discussed in a myriad ways in qualitative research reflecting interpretive, critical, and deconstructivist perspectives.

While there are many definitions of subjectivities out there, what has helped me think about subjectivities is the concept of subject positions. As human beings, we occupy various subject positions. For example, as a student, you might occupy the subject positions of being a daughter, a student, a mother, a sister, a wife, a career woman, etc. Each of these positions is connected to specific discourses of what it means for you to be connected to those labels, or subject positions. Perhaps there are ways in which you understand what it means to be a student, what is expected of you, and you either align with those expectations, modify those expectations, or resist some of those expectations and dismiss them. This would be termed as negotiating your position within the discourse of what it means to be a student.

In qualitative research, it is important to discuss these assumptions, beliefs, and values that inform the way you make meaning of your research topic. Claiming value neutrality would be intellectually dishonest because as human beings we have values, and if we became truly neutral and had no values, beliefs, or assumptions, we could argue that we would be quite robotic. And if a robot conducts an interview, it is unlikely that rich, detailed data would be gathered. Thus, qualitative researchers tend to be transparent about the values, beliefs, and assumptions with which they operate and how such things interact and inform their studies.

Often students confuse subjectivities with bias and equate them as synonymous terms. The former is a term associated with qualitative research and the latter with quantitative research. Because quantitative researchers work on measuring, capturing, and predicting truth well beyond coincidence levels, it is important in that kind of inquiry to ensure that they minimize errors and anything that would distort the path of measuring and capturing the truth. Therefore, they are careful about sample selection and instrument selection, and measure the accuracy of these selections through pre-established agreed upon rules. Any distortions in application of these rules could lead to skewing of the data and could reflect a bias, which would prevent the research from accomplishing its purpose. However, since qualitative researchers are in the business of understanding, interrogating, or deconstructing multiple truths, they are constantly thriving for gaining deep, rich, thick understanding buried within contextual details, social structures, discourses with which the participants identify and negotiate their experiences. How well a qualitative researcher can achieve depth of understanding is contingent on the relationship the researcher makes with the participants, the quality of data collection, and the researcher's analytical skills, informed by his or her positionality. All of these characteristics rely on the researcher's talents and skills, which are part and parcel of the researcher and cannot be situated within claims of value neutrality.

Therefore, in qualitative research, subjectivities are not used or understood the same way biases are used and understood in quantitative research. Since we cannot ever divorce ourselves from all the subject positions that shape us, qualitative research does not view subjectivities as negative influences on data. However, qualitative research calls for the researcher to become increasingly vigilant in order to reflect and address the role of subjectivities in research with academic rigor and trustworthiness.

The Subjective Self: Interactive Exercise

The first exercise is adapted from one that Jeff Rose[1] uses in his classes for students to understand epistemology and positionalities.

1. Draw a picture of something that is of great importance to you, or something that is a symbolic representation of what is of great importance to you. Do not worry about your artistic skills. You can draw stick figures, doodle, or anything that you please. If you find drawing to be not your cup of tea, create a collage with pictures, words, or objects. If you are more comfortable with digital form, then you could think of tools like Pinterest to clip images, words, anything that is of significance to you.
2. What is the story of this picture? What kinds of stories can be told about this picture or collection of pictures, words, objects?
3. Exchange your art with another student. Do not explain your art to your partner.
4. Ask your partner to tell you what they see in the picture, the meanings they make of your artwork.
5. Switch roles and tell your partner your perspective on their artwork.
6. Discuss with each other how your meaning making was aligned with what the intention was in the artwork.
7. Respond to the following prompts. You can use your researcher journal to respond to the prompts too, if there is not enough space underneath each prompt.

What were the most salient ways you tried to understand your partner's artwork? What stood out to you and why?

What were some clues that were present in the artwork that allowed you to construct a narrative or make meanings out of your partner's artwork?

What were some clues that were not present in the artwork, but still were useful to you (perhaps a prior experience, a similar shared event, etc.) in terms of framing a narrative or making meaning of your partner's artwork?

What can you say about the ways in which you processed the meanings/ narrative(s) of the artwork?

What views, beliefs, assumptions rose to the surface for you as a result of doing this activity?

The Eyes Are Watching: Interactive Exercise

Alan Peshkin (1988) presents various ways of understanding subjectivities in "In Search of Subjectivity—One's Own." Although he describes his category of subjective "I"s as discrete categories, I would argue that there are overlaps between those categories. I invite you to read the article to further your understanding of your subjectivities.

Think of three topics of research interest that appeal to you. You do not have to know all the empirical details of your interests. Just focus on the topics that appeal to you, and think of the reasons why you are drawn to these topics. Focus on which subjective Is match up best with each of your chosen topics. You can select the same Is multiple times or as many different Is as they appeal to you. There are no right or wrong answers, but what feels most correct to you. There are some cells that are left empty for you to fill in with other forms of subjective Is that are not listed in Peshkin's article but are present in your understanding of self.

TABLE 3.1

	Research Topic 1 (list topic below)	Research Topic 2 (list topic below)	Research Topic 3 (list topic below)
The Ethnic Maintenance I			
The Community Maintenance I			
The E Pluribus Unum I			
The Justice Seeking I			
The Pedagogical Meliorist I			
The Nonresearch Human I			

After reflecting on the various Is that you have selected, which research topic are you drawn to most? What helps you make the decisions? (The number of Is you have selected for the topic or the intensity of one kind of I that overwhelms the others, or something else?)

Instructor Note: If using this activity in class, you can also ask the students to reflect on theoretical framing of the research topics that are most connected to their subjectivities. Are the students operating from interpretive, critical, or deconstructive paradigms?

Student Note: If you are conducting this exercise on your own outside of class activities, reflect on whether your work is in the interpretive, critical, or deconstructive column. Does your research interest blur boundaries between the columns? Does your research interest distinctively fall into one column more than any other? What theoretical perspectives do you think align well with your research topic? Use your research journal to reflect on these questions.

Change Your Language, Change Your Paradigm

Often when people meet qualitative research for the first time, they try to understand concepts in qualitative research using terminologies from quantitative research. This usually causes confusion, and students have a hard time shifting their thinking. One of the best ways to shift your thinking is to immerse yourself in the language of qualitative inquiry and not try to understand it in terms of quantitative inquiry. In other words, you cannot try to understand how good a swimmer is if you continue to see the swimmer's performance in terms of a batting average. Sounds crazy, right? That is exactly what happens when you try to explain qualitative research using terminologies from quantitative research. It simply does not make any good sense.

Therefore, certain words used in quantitative research are not used in qualitative research in the same way or at all or used currently even if they were used in the past. I encourage you to incorporate a new vocabulary when doing qualitative research by not using the questionable words listed in Table 3.2. Although the terms appear side by side, they are not meant to be replacements for each other. Instead, the words on the right-hand side are commonly used words in qualitative research. I would advise getting a copy of Thomas Schwandt's (2007) *Dictionary of Qualitative Inquiry* for annotated definitions of the terms in the right-hand column. During the course of your qualitative studies, feel free to add more terms to the list below.

TABLE 3.2 Questionable and Acceptable Words/Phrases in Qualitative Inquiry

Questionable	Acceptable
Objective	Constructivist
Validity	Subjectivities
Reliability	Academic Rigor
Neutral	Trustworthiness
Generalizability	Transferability
Bias	Multiple Realities
Absolute Reality	Multiple Truths
Absolute Truth	Triangulation
Absolute Fact	Reflexivity
Completely True	Assumptions
Completely False	Beliefs

Insert your own words/phrases in the space below or in your journal as you continue learning about qualitative research.

TABLE 3.3 Questionable and Acceptable Words/Phrases in Qualitative Inquiry (Blank)

Questionable	Acceptable

Thinking about Research Purpose

Your research purpose can get a bit wordy and can possibly sound like a bit of a run-on sentence. Some things to keep in mind when considering a **research purpose** that is aligned with qualitative inquiry are:

Frame the research purpose in a way that **invites multiple possibilities** as a potential answer to the research purpose as opposed to one possible answer. For example, if you write a qualitative research purpose as, "The purpose of this study is to explore whether using iPads in the college classroom affects learning experiences," you have limited yourself to a finite possibility of answers. A research purpose such as this one would invite only two possible answers at the end of the study. Those answers would be limited to either iPads in the college classroom affect learning experiences or they do not affect learning experiences. This kind of framing is not conducive to in-depth inquiry.

Instead, consider a research purpose on the same topic as something like, "The purpose of this study is to explore the ways in which college students describe their learning experiences while using iPads in the classroom." This research purpose could also use further work such as adding how many participants, location of the study, etc. However, purely focusing on the structure of the purpose statement, this type of framing invites multiple possibilities as potential answers to the research purpose instead of limiting the research purpose to two finite answers. One of the ways in which you can frame the research purpose is by **reflecting on your intent** for the inquiry. Some verbs that can assist in this process are, but are not limited to:

- Explore
- Understand
- Investigate
- Identify
- Evaluate
- Describe
- Interrogate
- Deconstruct
- Negotiate

Once you have figured out the verb to use, you will have to **add contextual details.** Contextual details involve thinking about the context of the study, which includes you answering the following questions:

- How many participants?
- Where (use pseudonyms)?
- What will you explore? **Be specific** in identifying this, as your focus will sharpen here. For example, if you are interested in exploring the experiences of discrimination among Black female students at a predominantly White university, then say so instead of saying female students of color. If

exploring experience or perception, then the experience or perception of what exactly? **Be sharply focused.**

Avoid jargon as much as possible, and if you use jargon, then provide some definition about what might be your indicators for identifying what you are trying to explore. This is not to state that you have to have a way of counting or measuring some abstract concept. However, you have to draw some parameter around the scope of your study and what it is that you would be actually exploring and what might you use as potential indicators that align with what you are trying to explore. Even if you are critical or deconstructive in your approach, you still have to be able to discuss what it is that you would put at the other end of your gaze to explore, investigate, interrogate, or deconstruct.

Sorting Out Your Study: Interactive Exercise[2]

You have been exposed to various aspects of conceptualizing qualitative research. It is time to put all the ideas presented before in the context
of your work. Use the following prompts to reflect on your research interest.

List three areas of inquiry (topics of research) surrounding your potential
research interest:

1.

2.

3.

What do we know about these topics? List three key findings (broad, salient
points of conversation in the relevant literature).

1.

2.

3.

List 1–3 areas/topics/issues that could use further research.

1.

2.

3.

Hence, the study that can contribute to the literature could be:

Writing a Research Purpose: Interactive Exercise

Using the information presented in the previous section, start conceptualizing a research purpose.

What is the topic of your study?

Who would you talk to as participants in this study? How many participants will be part of your study?

What is the appropriate verb that reflects the intent of your inquiry and why? Which theoretical perspective are you aligning with when using that verb?

What is the context of this study—as in, where will the research take place? Is this an educational environment, a social environment, a digital environment, a familial environment?

Therefore, the purpose of your study is:

After you have completed writing a research purpose above, check the following:

- Is the research purpose open-ended to invite multiple possibilities as potential answers to the research purpose?
- Have you identified who the participants will be for your study?
- Have you stated the number of participants?
- Have you identified the site where the study will take place if appropriate?
- Have you used the verb that reflects most accurately your intent and theoretical perspective for this study?
- Have you used jargon sparingly?
- Have you used sharp, focused language to demonstrate accurately what it is that you want to study in an in-depth manner?

Thinking about Research Questions

Once you have completed writing your research purpose, you are then ready to conceptualize two to three research questions that align with your research purpose. Research questions are generally questions that break apart your research purpose more specifically to your focal points of inquiry. They give you a direction of what it is that you are going to study and keep you focused during data collection, analysis, and representation stages of your qualitative inquiry.

Some things to keep in mind when considering a **research question** that is aligned with qualitative inquiry are:

i. Make sure they **are aligned with the research purpose** that you created. It is common to write research questions that may be related to the research purpose but not fully aligned with the research purpose.

ii. One question can be the **conversion of the purpose statement into a question** if appropriate. For example, if the research purpose is specific about exploring experiences of X, your research question could be "What are the experiences of X?"

iii. Keep your **research questions simple.** Do not try to solve everything within the topic of your interest with complicated research questions. Pursue **one point of inquiry** in one question. If conducted with adequate depth, you will have complex, multilayered, sophisticated, and nuanced answers to the simplest of questions. It is your positionality (alignment of epistemology, ontology, theoretical, and methodological perspectives) that will bring you the depth and clarity you need to answer questions.

iv. **Limit the number of questions** you ask. The more questions you ask, the more you will have to answer. So, think carefully as to the number of questions you want to use for your study.

v. Ask questions that have **open-ended possibilities** for answers, such as:

    a. What are the experiences of . . .
    b. How does a participant describe X . . .
    c. In what ways does X play a role in Y?
    d. How does the participant identify X . . .

vi. Do not ask **closed-ended research** questions. Those are generally quantitative questions such as:

    a. Does this program benefit learning experiences of students?
    b. Do the participants like X more than Y?
    c. Does X cause Y?

vii. Research questions are topical **and should not contain the word "you,"** as in, "What are your experiences of X?" The mention of the word "you" makes it a direct question that is asked of a participant, which then becomes an interview question and not a research question exploring a topic of inquiry.

Here are some sample research purposes and questions:

Sample One

The purpose of the study is to explore the experiences of two graduates who credit their transition into alternative education from a traditional education setting in playing a role in their completion of high school in South Texas.
There are two research questions that this study will address:

1. In what ways do the participants describe their experiences in a traditional education setting prior to enrollment into an alternative education program?
2. In what ways do the participants describe their experiences in alternative education contributing to their graduation?

Sample Two

The purpose of this study is to conduct a Foucauldian power/knowledge analysis constructed from the perceptions of 15 teachers at an intermediate school in South Texas regarding the role of the teacher evaluation process and its influence on instructional practices.
Research questions that guide this study are:

1. What are the cultural, political, and strategic conditions encompassing the teacher evaluation process?
2. What relations and practices are enabled by the cultural, political, and strategic conditions of the teacher evaluation process?
3. What are the possibilities in the participants' behavioral changes in terms of the relationship between the evaluation process and pedagogy?

Writing Research Questions: Interactive Exercise

Copy your research purpose from the previous exercise in the space provided below.

What two or three areas can your topic be further broken down into for deeper and sharper inquiry?

What kinds of perspectives can the participant(s) in your study share about these subtopical areas?

Therefore, two research questions informing this study are:
1.

2.

After you have completed writing your research questions above, check the following:

1. Make sure that your research questions are aligned with your research purpose.
2. Make sure that your research questions are open-ended.
3. Make sure that your research questions are aligned with your theoretical perspective(s).
4. Make sure you have asked research questions and not interview questions.
5. Make sure that the questions reflect a realistic scope of what participants can provide if there are participants involved in your study.
6. Is the number of questions appropriate for your study?
7. Are the questions kept simple as they are worded, yet sharp in their focus?
8. Does each question pursue one line of inquiry, or could questions be split into two questions if two or more lines of inquiry are present in one question?

Data Sources in Qualitative Research

Almost anything can be considered data in qualitative research. Sources of information that after systematic (linear and nonlinear) review and analysis provide you with insights that answer your research purpose and questions and become evidence in your study. Data sources can be tangible sources of information that you can collect through active measures, such as interviews or observations, or through gathering relevant documents and archived materials. Data sources can also be intangible sources, such as memories, inspirations, insights, anything that helps you understand your study better. If you want to learn more about data sources that are not always tangible, I recommend reading Bettie St. Pierre's (1997) work on transgressive data. Also, if you are interested in thinking about the sites where you can collect data that are tangible and not so tangible, I recommend reading my work (Bhattacharya, 2009b) on this topic. You will find various ways of thinking of research sites from where you can gather information and how those sites are also connected to your theoretical and methodological perspective(s). For the purpose of this book, we will be focusing on tangible data sources. As you move forward in your understanding of qualitative research, I invite you to consider the possible sources of information that can be either tangible or tacit. Here is a list of tangible data sources for your reference, which is not exhaustive by any means.

Conversations/Interviews

Conversations/interviews occur in many forms in qualitative research. Conversations can be a form of interview that can range from informal chats to formal structured or semistructured open-ended interviews. The choice of data collection and the method of data collection should always be informed by your research purpose, questions, and theoretical perspective(s). For example, if your theoretical perspective was informed by Critical Race Theory (CRT), then your formal or informal interview questions should reflect the tenets of CRT in a way that is relevant to your study.

Observations

Observation stems out of conducting fieldwork in qualitative studies. Often fieldwork is associated with ethnographies, but observations are used as data sources for various types of qualitative studies that are not ethnographies. A common term, participant observation is used for not only discussing observation efforts in qualitative studies but also for discussing the level of participation in which the researcher engages. Various researchers have labeled the participatory roles a researcher might play ranging from minimally intrusive to being intensively engaged in the events one is attempting to observe. Regardless of whether a qualitative researcher is an active or passive participant in an event, the researcher is a participant in the environment that s/he is observing by being present in the environment. Observations can be conducted in public places, in specific research sites such as a classroom, or even in digital environments such as chatrooms, online forums, and virtual worlds.

Documents and Archived Materials

It is common in qualitative research to collect various types of relevant documents and archived materials that will provide the researcher a better contextual understanding. Some examples of documents include but are not limited to:

- Journals/diaries
- Newspaper citings
- Court papers
- Brochures
- Letters
- Pictures

Elicitations

An alternate way of knowing in qualitative research is elicitations. Elicitations are ways to create a context where the participant speaks about her experiences elicited by some sort of external trigger. This trigger could be pictures, objects, tasks, videos, lyrics, websites, etc. Either the participant identifies objects or pictures or triggers that are meaningful to her, or the researcher provides such triggers to the participant to generate conversations. For example, in my dissertation where I explored the experiences of international students in their first year in graduate school in the U.S., I asked the participants to take pictures of places, objects, or anything that reflected their experiences as international graduate students in their first year. Then, based on the pictures they took, we ran a digital slideshow and the participants discussed the reasons why they took the pictures, the ways in which the pictures spoke to their experiences, the discourses they were aligning with, modifying, and resisting. Some examples of elicitations are:

1. Photo elicitation
2. Object elicitation
3. Video elicitation
4. Lyric elicitation
5. Task elicitation

Find Your Data Sources: Interactive Exercise

Rewrite your research purpose once more so you can remind yourself of the specific details of the research purpose.

Would your study benefit from conversations? What kind of conversations would you like to have? Would they be formal, informal, structured, unstructured?

Would there be opportunities to observe any interactions that are occurring naturally? What kind of role would you play as a participant observer? What exactly would you observe and where?

What kinds of documents or archived materials would be relevant to provide further context for your study?

Would your study benefit from some participant-driven elicitation tasks? If so, what might they be? What would you like to know from those elicitations?

What kinds of questions do you have about your study at this point?

Golden Nuggets: Interactive Exercise

In this unit you have been introduced to how to conceptualize your research topic, how to write your research purpose and questions, and what to consider for tangible data sources in your qualitative study. Next is a scenario that will further sharpen your understanding of the ideas presented in this unit.

SCENARIO

I am interested in understanding how five ESL students in middle school in a midsouthern town in the U.S. make meaning of their experiences in ESL classrooms. Write a research purpose, two aligned research questions, and list possible sources of data collection informed by qualitative research methods.

Instructor Note: If you choose to conduct this nugget activity in class, then this could be a way to identify where there might be gaps in the students' understanding in conceptualizing a qualitative study and aligning the various parts of the study.

Student Note: If you choose to conduct this activity outside of your class assignment and find that you are struggling with certain areas, identify what those areas are, as that will help you identify the appropriate readings for you.

Notes

1   Exercise supplied by Jeff Rose, Davidson College, Davidson, North Carolina. Used with permission from Jeff Rose.
2   Adapted from instructional handout authored by Kathleen deMarrais (2004). Used with permission.

4
UNIT 4: WORKING WITH THEORETICAL FRAMEWORKS

In qualitative research, you position yourself well if you are fluent in theoretical perspectives such as positivism, postpositivism, phenomenology, critical theory, feminism, etc. This unit will offer you a chance to conceptualize these frameworks in a way that connects to your own research. I would recommend Crotty's (1998) text *The Foundations of Social Research: Meaning and Perspective in the Research Process* as the seminal text for this unit, as I am summarizing key ideas from that text in this unit.

Intentions of This Unit

In this unit, learners will be introduced to various theoretical perspectives and given opportunities to connect each of the theoretical perspectives to their research interests. Additionally, learners will be exposed to key tenets of each theoretical perspective, and assumptions that inform the perspective.

Positivism and Postpositivism

I group positivism and postpositivism in one section (although they are not the same) because as a qualitative researcher, you would be working from paradigms that extend beyond these two paradigms. However, it is important to have a sense of these two paradigms and their applicability to frame your understanding.

Positivism is a term that has historical roots in the works of Auguste Comte and Francis Bacon. Positivist perspectives usually rely on unambiguous and accurate knowledge of the world. Positivist inquiry relies on observation, often that is through scientific observation using methodologies that demonstrate a shared agreement between similar-minded scholars. While such an explanation would imply that there should be only one way of understanding positivism, Crotty (1998) reports that there are at least twelve varieties of positivism. However, in this unit, you will be presented an abbreviated variety of positivism. Comte discussed positivism beyond using mathematical terms to understand social patterns of human behavior via observation, experimentation, and comparison. The Vienna Circle of logical positivists relied more on mathematical functions and verifiability in positivism. So if I said that a cat had four legs, it was verifiable, as long as I was able to count the legs. For more abstract human behavior, verifiability was relegated to our senses and to carefully developed and agreed upon instrumentation.

From the 1990s and beyond, positivism became heavily reliant on mathematical functions and operated under the assumption that empirical scientific knowledge is both accurate and certain (Crotty, 1998, p. 27). This form of unified scientific knowledge created a binary between objective ways of knowing as scientific and subjective ways of knowing as unscientific. In other words, science does not bother with social construction of meaning. This way of thinking creates an artificial binary between value-neutral and value-driven research, when there is no clear way to really draw a line between such ideas.

Within **postpositivist** frameworks, physicists and other scholars raised concerns about the dogma about positivist approaches to scientific knowledge construction. Niels Bohr, a Nobel prize winner in physics, and Werner Heisenberg introduced the notion of uncertainty in scientific knowledge while studying subatomic particles and their movements. The notion of uncertainty introduced a chasm between what positivists aim to do and what is scientifically possible.

In addition, another postpositivist scholar, Sir Karl Popper, introduced the idea of falsification where a scientist can make a guess and find ways to make it false. And if the efforts to prove the guess false fail, then there is strength in the conjecture. Therefore, falsification became a process to determine the strength of a claim, that if a claim can withstand, despite efforts being made to falsify, then one can trust the claim to have merit, even if the claim cannot ever be 100 percent absolute. Thus, the scientific model of inquiry is to take a theory and convert it into a hypothesis, test the hypothesis, and find ways to prove it false. Popper introduced the idea that a theory or a hypothesis should remain open to refutation through scientific inquiry. Even if a theory or hypothesis can stand refutation, it can only be accepted as conditionally true, with the conditions specified and the degree of uncertainty accounted for in the final claim. The essence of Popper's claim of scientific statement is that every one of them is "tentative forever" (Crotty, 1998, p. 32).

Thomas Kuhn introduced the idea of paradigm and paradigm shift when discussing scientific inquiry. He stated that all scientists operate from a theoretical background that reflects the scientist's understanding about knowledge and inquiry. However, if during inquiry, findings exceed the parameters of the paradigm, then there is a crisis. A scientist can then try to force fit the findings into an existing paradigm or be open to new ways of understanding, thereby causing a paradigm shift. Kuhn's ideas about science and scientific inquiry, then, not only creates space for uncertainty, but subjectively situates the researcher within certain paradigms that are only stable until new evidence is presented to contest the boundaries of the paradigm.

Feyerabend, another postpositivist scholar, did not approve of the absolutist stance of positivism and introduced the notion of a pluralistic methodology because he identified science and every other way of knowing a set of beliefs with its own associated mechanisms of inquiry. He positioned science as a messy enterprise instead of the appearance of being neat, rational, and absolute. Feyerabend called for identifying the value of what might appear to be messy, chaotic, or sloppy, as that might lead to critical scientific discoveries.

What the postpositivist scholars created was a discursive space that questioned the ahistorical, acultural, value-neutral understanding of reality and scientific inquiry. These ideas have created room for constructionist views of meaning making and reality. Those who align with positivism now remain cautious about what they claim, as their findings and the degree of certainty they ascribe to that claim as ideas now remain open to falsification, and any claim of 100 percent certainty is vulnerable to one study finding a contrary outcome. If nothing else, the postpositivists made a significant impact in challenging the positivist stance of complete objectivity and certainty.

Interpretivism

Like positivism, there are various theoretical perspectives that could be considered under the big banner of interpretivism. However, it would be beyond the scope of this book to discuss all of them. Instead we will discuss key perspectives within this framework.

Interpretivism came out of the need to have a way to understand the social world that is not limited by the tenets of positivism. Unlike positivism, interpretivism takes into account the cultural and historical interpretations of one's social world when conducting inquiry. Max Weber has been credited for being one of the pioneers of interpretivism. He favored human sciences that focused on understanding instead of developing causal explanations. William Dilthey furthered Max Weber's position by stating that human social realities require different means of inquiry than perhaps what positivists in natural sciences might inquire. Wilhelm Windelband added a twist to how scholars understood interpretivism. He posited that natural sciences were focused on developing generalized laws and patterns whereas culturally and historically situated studies were concerned about in-depth individualized understanding.

Interpretivism has been a broad term that can be split into various specified frameworks. Here, we will discuss three types of interpretive orientation to social science research. These three types are: symbolic interactionism, phenomenology, and hermeneutics. While there are several volumes of books written individually on these three historical streams of interpretivism, in this book you will be introduced to the key abbreviated ideas.

Symbolic Interactionism

Herbert Blumer, a student of George Herbert Mead, is often credited for pioneering knowledge about symbolic interactionism. He was strongly influenced by Mead's earlier work on constructionism. Blumer stated that because individuals make meaning of objects based on their own understanding of the objects, any acts towards objects, things, events, and interactions are informed by the meaning an individual makes. Blumer emphasized that social interactions inform choices humans make when making meaning of their worlds, events, objects, etc. Additionally, Blumer stated that the meaning-making process is an interpretive process where individuals are continuously modifying their understanding as needed based on their interactions. The symbolic part of this framework was entirely contingent on what the individuals deemed to be symbolic, tangible, or otherwise with which the individual interacted and made meaning. Symbols can include whatever has significant meaning for the participant. These could include, but are not limited to, language, dialogues, policies, anything with which the participant interacts that creates meaning.

In the following section, you will find an abbreviated list that summarizes information presented thus far about symbolic interactionism. This abbreviated list will allow you to gain some focus on the key ideas of symbolic interactionism.

Emphasis of Symbolic Interactionism

- Explains how interactions with tangible and intangible symbols create meaning in people's lived experiences.
- An understanding how people see themselves, others, and how they think others perceive them.
- Understanding social reality as experienced by participants while they make meaning of their interactions with their world.

Tenets and Assumptions

- Humans act toward things on the basis of meanings these things have for them.
- Meaning of such things is derived from social interactions of one with others.

Selected Major Scholars/Schools of Thought

- Mead (1883–1931)—sociologist, psychologist, advocated pragmatism, focused on the development of self and discovering some objective way of knowing the social world; focused on the dynamic ways in which the actor interacted with the social world and made interpretations.

- Blumer (1900–1987)—(Mead's student), extended Mead's ideas in symbolic interactionism by adding meaning, language, and thought to how people know, understand, interact, and navigate their social world.
- Goffman (1922–1982)—sociologist, influenced by Blumer, attempted to find patterns in human behavior; promoted a dramaturgical presentation of self, as in being observers of the theatrical events of our lives.
- Howard Becker (1928–)—considered part of the Chicago School of Sociology (see below), focused heavily on qualitative analysis of data, known for his work in sociology of deviance, art, and his guidance of others in the practice of sociology.
- Chicago School—one of the oldest, most prestigious sociology departments, early specialization in urban sociology and ethnographic fieldwork; known for the development of symbolic interactionist approach; focused on the development of patterns in human behavior informed by social or environmental triggers.

Selected Methodologies Used by Symbolic Interactionists

- Ethnography
- Performative approaches
- Autoethnography
- Interview studies
- Case studies
- Arts-based approaches

Selected Critiques of Symbolic Interactionism

- Needs to acknowledge the blurring of the researcher and the researched in various methodological spaces despite the intention of the researcher to document events from the perspective of the participant.
- Difficult to claim that a voice of the participant has been captured since the voice and the narratives are co-constructed.
- Unable to make any holistic understanding of any meaning-making processes because the understanding is transient for the moments in which data were collected, analyzed, and interpreted.

Symbolic Interactionism and Your Research Interest: Interactive Exercise

Recall my wiki research focused on the graduate students' learning experiences when working with wiki within the context of a qualitative research class. If I were to conceptualize the inquiry through a symbolic interactionist lens, I would reframe my research question as the following:

How do graduate students in qualitative research classes make meaning of the use of wikis in their classes in relation to their learning experiences?

One can argue with appropriate context leading up to the above research question that it can be seen as a symbolic interactionist question because there could be significant meaning-making processes embedded within the students' interactions with the wikis while learning the content of qualitative inquiry. Such a question is still grounded within the constructionist epistemology and aligns with Blumer's interactionist assumptions, such as actions towards symbols are based on the meanings individuals make about them, meaning making is a process of social interaction, and meaning making can be modified through the process of interpretation and interaction by the individual.

Now, keeping the abovementioned strategies in mind, what would your research question look like if you informed your research interest through symbolic interactionism?

Using the tenets of symbolic interactionism (significant meaning-rich symbol, interaction with symbol, modification and interpretations of meaning), list how your research question aligns with the tenets.

TABLE 4.1

Tenets of Symbolic Interactionism	Evidence of Tenet in Research Question

Phenomenology

One of the key originating ideas of phenomenology is that if we had experienced a phenomenon in our past, as we recall our experiences, then perhaps we can find possibilities for new ways of understanding those experiences through making new meanings and gaining new insights. Central to this notion is the idea of intentionality. Intentionality should be understood as a different concept than the regular use of the word "intentions." Intentionality refers to the relationship between the observer and the observed, or in other words, the subject and the object, or the ways in which people connect meaningfully with the world. The argument put forward is that the observer and observed are not apart from each other but interconnected.

Phenomenological scholars encourage an inquiry that investigates the meaning making of the structure of the phenomenological experience. In phenomenology, scholars can "engage with phenomena in our world and make sense of them directly and immediately" (Crotty, 1998, p. 79). To combat the prior experiences of an individual, phenomenological scholars (Heron, 1967; Husserl, 1931; Marton, 1986; Sadler, 1969; Spigelberg, 1982; Wolff, 1984) recommend that we bracket our prior understandings so that we can see and/or understand the phenomenon in new and undiscovered ways. The criticism for bracketing has been that it might never really be possible for one to really claim a pure compartmentalization of one's prior knowledge and subjectivities to such an extent that there can be no influence on the meaning-making processes during inquiry.

Crotty (1998) offers an informative account of how phenomenology is practiced in North America compared to how it was conceptualized outside North America. The documenting of subjective experience through bracketing, understanding the meanings from the perspective of the participants, letting cultural understandings prevail is different from the original spirit of phenomenology that called for a critical understanding of cultural meaning-making processes to unveil fresh understanding and meaning of a phenomenon as experienced by individuals. In North American discourses, the assumption is that if studied thoroughly, one can identify an invariant theme or the essence of experiencing a phenomenon among participants. However, recently scholars (Vagle & Hofsess, 2016) have challenged the notion of finding "essence" and have argued that one can conduct phenomenological work more generatively, looking for possibilities instead of a fixed essence.

In the following section, you will find an abbreviated list that summarizes information presented thus far about phenomenology. This abbreviated list will allow you to gain some focus on the key ideas of phenomenology.

Emphasis of Phenomenology

- Accounts for people's understanding of their lived experience of a phenomenon.
- Focuses on lived experiences of a phenomenon.
- Questions the meaning made of the phenomenon being experienced.
- Essence of the shared experiences of the phenomenon.

Tenets and Assumptions

- There is a fixed essence to a lived experience of a phenomenon.
- The meaning of experiencing a phenomenon can be captured through lived experiences.
- Prior cultural experiences could interfere with meaning making.

Selected Major Scholars/Schools of Thought

- Edmund Husserl (1859–1938)—understood that studying the structure of consciousness requires investigating the phenomena upon which consciousness was focused; proposed such investigation through bracketing the researcher's assumptions about the existing world to identify essences of experience through a process called epoché.
- Martin Heidegger (1889–1976)—focused on the state of being and unveiling of the state of being to discover fresh meanings, not clouded by normative discourses of culture.
- Clark Moustakas (1923–2012)—a phenomenological methodologist offering other ideas about data reduction, invariant theme identification, and discovering essence.
- Amedeo Giorgi (1926–)—was initially an experimental psychologist, but was not able to answer the questions through experimental psychology and therefore explored phenomenology. His understanding of qualitative methods deepened, and he developed the descriptive phenomenological method in psychology influenced by Husserl and Merleau-Ponty.
- van Kaam (1920–2007)—influenced the work of Giorgi; organized the graduate program at Duquesne University on phenomenological psychology; explored the essence of one's feelings of an experienced phenomenon as the primary focus of his dissertation and extended his work to intersect the tenets of phenomenology and psychology.

Selected Methodologies Used by Phenomenologists

- Phenomenological hermeneutics
- Descriptive phenomenology
- Studies of essence

Selected Critiques of Phenomenology

- Essence may not be single or fixed. There could be multiple essences.
- Might never get to one single essence.
- Cultural critique is missing, and focus on phenomenon is not always present in studies conducted.
- Difficult to claim bracketing experiences to be anything more than reflexivity.

Phenomenology and Your Research Interest: Interactive Exercise

Recall my wiki research focused on the graduate students' learning experiences when working with wiki within the context of a qualitative research class. If I were to conceptualize the inquiry through a phenomenological lens, I would reframe my research question as the following:

What might be the ways in which participants' experiences demonstrate a meaningful connection with the content taught in an introductory graduate-level qualitative research class while exploring the phenomenon of using wikis for class assignments?

The previous question can be justified as a phenomenological question due to various reasons. Remember your work is only as strong as your academic justifications. I could argue that I am exploring an invariant theme, an essence of experiencing a phenomenon in the above question. Or I could argue that there could be multiple lines of flight to discover the possibilities of meaningful connections. But it is certainly key to identify what we would consider as a phenomenon. Once Wikipedia was introduced in the digital world, it has become a phenomenon. Attempting to expose students to the construction of the wikis is a fertile space for students to explore meaning on an individualistic level and also on the level of the cultural understanding of wikis. As a researcher, if I want to situate my study more along the lines of Husserl's work, then I would try to specifically take a critical perspective of the current use and understanding of wikis and attempt to explore the data in a way that might not always align with the established understanding of wikis. Additionally, if I want to position myself within a hybridized version of phenomenology, blending Husserl's philosophy and the North American evolution of phenomenology, I might be interested in understanding my subjectivity, data reduction, and attempt to put myself in the participants' shoes and understand their perspectives as much as possible. And if I want to take a more poststructural approach to phenomenological work, then I might look into Vagle's approach of post-intentionality when developing the research design. Eventually, I need to document how I am situating myself within the discourse of the evolution of phenomenology from its inception and how my research design is aligned with my understanding.

Now, keeping the abovementioned strategies in mind, what would your research question look like if you informed your research interest through phenomenology?

Using the tenets of phenomenology (intentionality, cultural critique, identification of phenomenon, tenets from the North American transformation of the field), list how your research question aligns with the tenets.

TABLE 4.2

Tenets of Phenomenology	*Evidence of Tenet in Research Question*

Hermeneutics

Hermeneutics has its historical roots in interpreting biblical texts. However, over time, the practice of textual analysis not only extended to non-biblical texts but also to "human practices, human events, human situations—in an attempt to 'read' these in ways that bring understanding" (Crotty, 1998, p. 87). Such expansion of the scope of hermeneutics was possible because we use language in our social interactions, and due to our specific ways in which we use language, we not only have differing encounters but also make meaning of our encounters differently.

Specifically, hermeneutics assumes a connection between the reader and the text that drives the interpretation. Taking this assumption further, it can also be argued that the author of a text can make connections to readers in various situations through the interaction of the reader and the author's text. In this way, hermeneutics can have the implications of creating shared meaning between communities or people.

The process of using hermeneutic theory to analyze texts aims to explore a deeper understanding of the text than what is readily present in the writing, or what seems like easily accessible intent of the author. Given that languaged thoughts are embedded with assumptions and context, a systematic hermeneutic inquiry might create an in-depth understanding of a meaning of the text that is not readily transparent. Another value of hermeneutic work is that through deeper analysis, researchers can explore and postulate assumptions made in languaged ideas. Identifying grounding assumptions has implications for a different kind of relationship between the author and the reader than a straightforward reading of a text.

One key idea within the discourse of hermeneutics is the notion of hermeneutic circle. Hermeneutic circle refers to starting with an idea and developing the idea with depth and understanding to create even deeper and more amplified understanding of the original idea, thereby coming to a full circle. This process of creating this circle of understanding also emphasizes the value of working on smaller parts of an idea with the intent of gaining an in-depth understanding of the whole. However, such an assumption is not without its problem when studying human behavior. Can human beings or their actions or behaviors be understood as a whole? Would it not be only an expression of the relationship between the researcher and what is being researched? Yet in analyzing texts, deeper understanding can occur if the analyzer can switch between seeing the trees from the forest and can shuttle in between seeing the whole and the parts as needed.

Such shuttling between the part and the whole can be accomplished through being an empathic reader, according to one of the key scholars of hermeneutics, Friedrich Schleiermacher. He suggested that reading and analyzing texts are not just exercises with prescriptive steps for in-depth understanding. Instead, such a process is similar to being a good listener with an attempt to put oneself in the speaker's position. In this way hermeneutics could at once be a close analysis of how words are organized, how sentences are structured, how emotions and intentions are conveyed. On the other hand, seeing the context in which ideas are communicated and how they are communicated would be akin to seeing the whole constituted of its parts. This bidirectional movement between the parts and the whole is what strengthens hermeneutic inquiry. In addition to analyzing texts in parts and whole, hermeneutic scholars value situating the text and the author in their social, historical, and cultural contexts as our lived experiences are not occurring in a vacuum nor are our ways of understanding and making meaning of them, whether we talk about them verbally or write about them in text. In this way the hermeneutic circle is conceptualized as the analysis moves from the individual to a contextualized world back to the individual again with a stronger and amplified understanding.

In the following section you will find an abbreviated list that summarizes information presented thus far about hermeneutics. This abbreviated list will allow you to gain some focus on the key ideas of hermeneutics.

Emphasis of Hermeneutics

*   Making meaning of texts.
*   Find implicit meanings and make those meanings explicit.
*   A way to understand others and by extension ourselves. It becomes a study of understanding how human beings choose to express themselves.
*   Language is the central focus.
*   Attempt to amplify understanding through expanding the hermeneutic circle, bringing the past and the present to consciousness through understanding, exploring understanding ontologically allowing the state of being to come to the forefront.

Tenets and Assumptions

*   There are inherent implicit and explicit meanings embedded in text that can be analyzed and represented as findings.
*   The researcher can make explicit assumptions made in the text by the author that the author might be unaware of or did not make explicit.
*   There has to be a relationship between the parts and the whole and a movement between the parts and the whole.
*   Author's social and cultural history has a role in how texts are produced.
*   Interpretation of text builds a bridge between the past tradition and the present (Gadamer).
*   Hermeneutics is a process of phenomenological seeing (Heidegger).
*   With an expansion of the hermeneutic circle through increased amplified understanding where the interpreter's own beliefs and values are marginalized, an objective account of the world can be obtained (Dilthey).

Selected Major Scholars/Schools of Thought

- Friedrich Schleiermacher (1768–1834)—strong background in theology and created discourses to reconcile ideas borne out of Enlightenment and traditional Protestant Christianity. Explored and expanded the nature of understanding from biblical texts to non-biblical texts, and other modes of communication.
- Georg Anton Friedrich Ast (1778–1841)—focused on philosophical hermeneutics and was part of the hermeneutic circle.
- William Dilthey (1833–1911)—related interpretation to historical objectification, with the hopes that if the researcher could keep his/her ideas and values outside of the inquiry, understanding could be extended to the hermeneutic circle in an amplified manner, and in repeating this process, some broad patterns could be identified.
- Martin Heidegger (1879–1976)—focused on the state of being unveiling and advocated a phenomenological seeing of the interaction between the text, the author, and the researcher.
- Hans-Georg Gadamer (1900–2002)—focused on fusion of past traditions and present through interpretive understanding acting as a bridge.

Selected Methodologies

- Phenomenological hermeneutics
- Descriptive phenomenology
- Reading theory studies
- Literary criticism

Selected Critiques of Hermeneutics

- Interpretation is limited to the extent the researcher can achieve depth of understanding and will always be subjective.
- The concept of parts and whole can be problematic because there is no universally agreed upon ways to claim wholeness and therefore any interpretation is always situated with the researcher's understanding of the big and the small picture.

Hermeneutics and Your Research Interest: Interactive Exercise

Recall my wiki research focused on the graduate students' learning experiences when working with wiki within the context of a qualitative research class. If I were to conceptualize the inquiry through a hermeneutic focus, I would reframe my research question as the following:

How do the authors of wiki articles demonstrate their interaction with the content of qualitative methods based on their exposure to the content in graduate-level qualitative methods classes?

The previous question can be justified as a hermeneutically informed question because the object of analysis would be the wiki content, which is a mostly text-based work with some pictures. Additionally, in the question I am seeking to explore the relationship between the text and the author. If conducted, I would have interviewed the authors to further deepen my understanding of the authors' social, cultural, and historical contexts (fusion of past and present horizons) of learning qualitative methods and using wikis. Finally, if I was inspired in Heidegger's approach to hermeneutics, or the phenomenology of seeing, then I would contemplate on the existential structures and allow my state of being to come to the forefront to bring further understanding of the text and the authors' states of being.

Now, keeping the abovementioned strategies in mind, what would your research question look like if you informed your research interest through hermeneutics?

Using the tenets of hermeneutics (interaction between the text and the author, hermeneutic circle, parts and whole, existential structures, ontological exploration, fusion of past and present horizons), list how your research question aligns with the tenets.

TABLE 4.3

Tenets of Hermeneutics	Evidence of Tenet in Research Question

Critical Theories

Like every other theoretical perspective discussed so far, I will limit the discussion of critical theories to a selected few while inviting the readers to conduct their own exploration into their chosen perspectives. Generally, critical theories focus on the role of the social structures of oppression playing out through the lived experiences of people. The focus of oppression could be something singular or intersected categories. Singular categories could include class, whereas intersected categories could include race, class, and gender. However, most studies conducted through a critical perspective often are at an intersection of multiple categories.

Depending on who you ask, some might put deconstructive perspectives as critical theories whereas others speak of them as critiques of some established theoretical perspective. For example, postmodernism can be seen as a critique of modernism, poststructuralism can be seen as a critique of structuralism, and postcolonialism a critique of colonialism, and so on. The purpose of deconstructive perspectives is to break apart foundational assumptions so that from the ruins of what is broken something else can be constructed. What that something else is, is open to multiple options, which are also open to further deconstructions.

In the next section, I discuss Critical Race Theory and feminism so that you can understand how some of the discourses around critical theory inform qualitative inquiry. Please explore further into the wide spectrum of critical and deconstructive perspectives for other theories if they are of interest to you.

Critical Race Theory

Considered the founder of Critical Race Theory (CRT), Derrick Bell Jr. highlighted the inequities of race from minority perspectives in the U.S. Later, intersections between race, class, gender, access to other resources, such as legal and property rights, were highlighted by other scholars (Ladson-Billings, 1998; Ladson-Billings & Tate, 1995). While Derrick Bell's background was African American, another prominent scholar, Alan Freeman (who was White) was credited with creating similar concerns about the slow-paced improvement of race reform. The primary premise of CRT is that racism is a pervasive part of American culture and it is not an aberrant occurrence. Instead, the reason why racism might feel absent or normalized is because of how common it is in so many aspects in people's lives (Delgado, 2000) in big and small ways. Originally, CRT came out of the discussions of its predecessor, critical legal studies, where not enough efforts were made to openly disavow the various forms of inequities that were operational daily in the lives of minorities in the U.S. Many scholars of color felt the need to critique the existing social structures in terms of how poorly it handled issues of racism. Thus, emerged CRT to address some difficult issues around race, more directly than the ways in which critical legal studies engaged in these issues.

Another reason CRT moved away from critical legal studies is because of scholars who advocated for CRT, valued storytelling as a way to document myths, truths, assumptions, and wisdom of Blacks and minorities otherwise not possible through critical legal studies (Delgado, 2000). Experiential knowledge and shared history with each other were given space for dialoguing. Gloria Ladson-Billings (1998) elaborates that the reason for the emergence of CRT was the dissatisfaction with liberal approaches to pull up people slowly from where they were. This was a slow-paced improvement where many people continued to suffer, and some radical transformation and actions were needed. In addition, with affirmative actions, many White women were benefitted through employment and other opportunities, which highlighted strongly that racial inequity existed as a large barrier to ethnic minorities (Ladson-Billings, 1998).

Thus, the primary thrust of CRT studies is a systematic inquiry about how racial inequities are created and sustained in the lives of ethnic minorities in U.S. These studies cover many areas such as social science, education, and law, and offer tangible data that show the clear divide in opportunities, access, and resources. As more and more scholars practiced CRT, storytelling began to take a primary form of building knowledge where people were able to name their reality (Delgado, 2000). The strength of storytelling was a recognition that people's construction of reality differs and a space needs to be created to acknowledge this variation instead of a dominant narrative or a dominant group narrating truths of about a minority group. Thus, by allowing storytelling, a group can thoroughly reflect on its strengths, weaknesses, areas of needs, areas of strengths, and connect to their own ways of knowing and being through revisiting memories and their ways of making meaning of them. This also allowed for counternarratives to emerge that challenged dominant, ethnocentric narratives.

In the following section, you will find an abbreviated list that summarizes information presented thus far about CRT. This abbreviated list will allow you to gain some focus on the key ideas of CRT.

Emphasis of Critical Race Theory

- Creates awareness of social structures of oppression that manifest in people's lived experiences, especially in the experiences of African Americans and people of color.
- Interrogates institutional structures that promote oppressive discourses and social inequalities and demonstrates intersections with other social structures of oppression.
- Examines how inequities are sustained and proliferated by oppressive social structures and ideologies.
- Corrects social injustices through interrogation, awareness, policy changes, etc.

- Eradicates oppression.
- Creates transformational learning to create critical consciousness.

Tenets and Assumptions

- Racism is common and not aberrational, and thus dominant ideologies should be challenged routinely.
- The incentive to eradicate racism is not the same for everyone, and therefore as pervasive as it is, it is not something that everyone aims to correct.
- Social construction of race creates the ways in which people experience and understand racism.
- Discourses about minority groups are reflections of the current economic and labor needs.
- Counternarrative and storytelling offer a space for voices that are otherwise absent, thus legitimizing experiential knowledge.

Selected Major Scholars/Schools of Thought

- Derrick Bell (1930–2011)—founder of Critical Race Theory; offered strong analysis of the sustenance of inequities based on Brown vs. Board decision; offered critiques of traditional civil rights discourse.
- Richard Delgado (1939–)—a prolific scholar of CRT and the legal systems; shaped the pioneering of CRT. He questioned and critiqued the ways in which free speech functioned and integrated storytelling into the workings of the law.
- Gloria Ladson-Billings (1947–)—a strong advocate of CRT in education. She is a scholar and a teacher educator and conceptualized culturally relevant pedagogy emerging out of her understanding of Critical Race Theory.
- William Tate—A strong advocate of educational reform, colleague of Ladson-Billings (have published seminal pieces together), focuses on CRT and education, especially in STEM areas, with documented focus on African American males and African Americans.

Selected Methodologies Used by Critical Race Theorists

- Critical ethnography
- Critical incident methodology
- Critical case study
- Biographical study
- Oral history
- Critical autoethnography
- Critical narrative inquiry/storytelling

Selected Critiques of CRT

- Multipronged solutions are hard to implement.
- Cultural outsiders who conduct CRT might only be able to identify solutions from the researcher's perspective.
- Solutions can be seen as being presumptuous to knowing what a marginalized group might need even when the researcher is a cultural insider.
- Not all cultural insiders are equally focused on inequities.

Critical Race Theory and Your Research Interest: Interactive Exercise

Recall my wiki research focused on the graduate students' learning experiences when working with wiki within the context of a qualitative research class. If I were to conceptualize the inquiry through a CRT focus, I would reframe my research question as the following:

How do the formal and informal structures of higher education respond to the needs of students of ethnic minority backgrounds as they attempt to become technology literate in their graduate education in a predominantly White institution?

> The previous question can be justified as a question informed by CRT because it sets up the question to interrogate both formal and informal structures of education and access to resources, support systems, campus organizations that students of ethnic background might be able to use as they learn how to become more technology literate. The assumptions leading to such a question could be that in a predominantly White institution, how students of ethnic backgrounds navigate and negotiate their available support system is worthy of exploration to either challenge a dominant structure of inequity, and/or provide counternarratives of students successfully navigating in an environment where they are visibly a minority, with risks of feeling isolated and lacking a sense of belongingness.

Now, keeping the abovementioned strategies in mind, what would your research question look like if you informed your research interest through CRT?

Using the tenets of CRT (challenge dominant ideology, evoke storytelling, systematic exploration of inequities, oppressive structures, pervasive forms of racism), list how your research question aligns with the tenets.

TABLE 4.4

Tenets of CRT	Evidence of Tenet in Research Question

Feminism

Similar to the previous sections, it would be beyond the scope of this book to discuss all the different forms of feminisms that are out there. Needless to say, there are volumes of books, series, and journal articles that cover the field of feminism with more efficiency than I could in this space. In the next section, I introduce you to a few types of feminism and invite you to explore anything I did not mention on your own.

Liberal Feminism

Liberal feminism is grounded in an individualistic understanding of feminism where discussions of equality are driven by the individual's actions in society. In other words, liberal feminists would fight against any broad form of generalization of women being inferior, less capable of performing or doing some task, and argue for treating each individual woman based on her abilities, choices, and actions, and as an overly generalized category. Often liberal feminists might look for the government to protect everyone through laws for equal rights and opportunities, but also require the government to interfere as less as possible in the lives of people, especially women.

Generally speaking, in the U.S., during the Civil Rights Movement in the 1960s, in addition to the realization of racial discrimination, women began to identify gender discrimination too. Therefore, several groups emerged to advocate for women so that issues of gender discrimination could be brought to light. Often, the popular understanding of feminism is a limited and reductive understanding of feminism that came out of this wave of feminism. Women's rights movements started with laws and reform to bring forward equal rights to all human beings. In many ways, liberal feminism was quite humanist in nature. Issues on which liberal feminists focused were reproduction, reproductive rights and abortion access, income, sexual harassment, voting, work, affordable health care and childcare, and violence against women.

Marxist Feminism

Feminists who identify with this group are more focused on the inequities generated due to class structure in our society. Thus, these feminists call for a radical change in the class structure so that the inequities can be addressed effectively. So, if this group of feminists were to speak to the liberal feminists, then they would state that no level of individual equality can be achieved if our society is divided into class structures with the kind of divide that exists between the rich, middle, and poor classes. Understandably, Marxist feminists focus on work, employment, paid work, and unpaid work at home. One of the ideas this group of feminists produced is that domestic work should not just be a woman's domain, but shared between a woman and her partner. Otherwise, women who are working at home and working outside are carrying double the workload but not getting compensated proportionately.

The foundation of Marxist feminism can be found in the works of Karl Marx (of course), but also in the works of Friedrich Engels (1884/2010), especially in *The Origin of the Family, Private Property, and the State*. Engel criticizes the nuclear family as being an oppressive structure for women where she remains subordinated, not because she is less capable, intelligent, or inferior in any way to a man, but because her labor and sexual faculties are being controlled by a patriarchal system. He criticized the notion of holding women to some sexual morality, punished when they commit adultery, and placing them submissive to their husbands. Historically, tracing back to the need to control a group of human beings as women were being controlled in the 1800s when Engels wrote his book, he compared the treatment of women to patriarchs owning slaves.

Radical Feminism

This group of feminists strongly believes that all forms of oppression can be best understood if oppression of women is understood in its depth. They propose that oppression of women is one of the oldest forms of oppression and one that runs the deepest in our social fabric. Their understanding of the kind of oppression that women share also forwards the argument that it is unlikely that men could really understand this kind of oppression and at the depth at which women experience and live such oppression daily.

Such specialized ways of thinking about women's oppression for this group of feminists caused them to separate and focus on issues that are exclusive to female or women culture. However, please note, not all radical feminists will align with the above explanation, nor have they ALL separated, but the common trend shared among most radical feminists are women's sexuality and reproductive issues. Thus this group of feminists focuses on issues such as prostitution, rape, sexual harassment, pornography, abortion, domestic violence, and battering.

The issues raised by this group of feminists highlight how even with class issues and individual autonomous issues addressed, what remains the big elephant in the room is the pervasive ways in which patriarchy works. Therefore, unless patriarchy is completely erased, this group of feminists does not see any kind of equality for women in any way that is sustainable. Patriarchy is conceptualized as the intricate and interconnected system of power that sustains male supremacy to suppress women. Of specific concern for this group of feminists were traditional gender roles and they called for complete abandonment of any connection with what women do and equating their abilities to a limited understanding of gender or gender roles. The argument presented forward was that women are not a simple category with which they can be disciplined and limited to only certain acts because of their gender. Instead, women represented diversity and therefore cannot be easily grouped into one or two traditional roles and attempts made to limit women to any roles while preventing them from engaging in other roles should be stopped.

Situated and Critical Feminisms

Black feminism, Latina and Chicana feminism, postmodern feminism, postcolonial feminism, transnational feminism, and Asian feminism are just broad examples of situated and critical feminism. These groups are focused on more specialized analysis of social structures of oppression as they relate to the experiences and subjectivities of the members in the group. For example, Black feminism focuses on how social structures of oppression play out in subjugating Black men and women. Please note that many feminists would argue that patriarchy hurts both men and women because it is a limiting discourse for everyone as it restricts people to gender roles. Thus Black feminism and many other situated feminisms explore the ways in which oppression exists at the intersection of race, class, gender, and other relevant categories. bell hooks (1990) has been extremely vocal about issues of concern to the Black community that need to be understood within its local and national contexts. For example, hooks raises the issue that since Black males do not have equality with White males, equality for Black women is not the same as equality for their White women counterparts. Additionally, bell hooks does not exclude men from feminism as other groups might (especially radical feminists). She speaks of men as comrades working together with women to erase social structures of oppression.

Similarly, Latina and Chicana feminists raise issues that are specific to their community and analyze how social structures of oppression play out in their everyday lives. Gloria Anzaldúa (1999) raised the issue of mestiza consciousness to help understand how social structures of oppression play out in the lives of those who have mixed ancestry and the continuous shuttling between the physical and psychological borders in which the mestiza people engage.

Postmodern and postcolonial feminism offer critiques of modernist and colonial discourses embedded in patriarchy that affect how we understand and take up various subject positions in our everyday lives. Both of these types of feminisms use deconstructive tools to break apart dominant narratives in our society, otherwise known as grand narratives, so that other possibilities could be identified. Moreover, feminists in these groups are especially conscious about the binary relationships formed when we create a line of division between two ideas, concepts, or groups of people and hierarchically organize the two groups. For example, Us versus Them, Citizen versus Alien, White versus Other.

Transnational feminists look at the ways in which human capital is moved from one part of the globe to another and the effect it has on the human beings as part of the move, especially women. Some scholars (Grewal & Kaplan, 1994) have also intersected transnationalism with postmodern critiques to deconstruct global grand narratives. These feminists also explore and analyze the effects of migration, global labor laws, and local immigration laws to closely interrogate various social systems of power that intersect with patriarchy and create multiple social structures of oppression.

In the following section you will find an abbreviated list that summarizes information presented thus far about feminism. This abbreviated list will allow you to gain some focus on the key ideas of feminism.

Emphasis of Feminism

- Breaking apart and recreating a man-made world.
- Critique of patriarchy and other social structures that support patriarchy.
- Struggle for equity and liberation for women on all fronts of life.
- Freeing of human possibilities through struggle against culturally imposed stereotypes, sexuality, responsibilities.
- Politics directed at changing existing relations between men and women in society.
- Explore how patriarchy works with other social structures of oppression, locally, nationally, and globally.
- Break any social structure of oppression that hierarchically organizes people and puts labels on human beings that makes them Other.
- Resist essentialization for the purpose of disciplining and silencing of activist voices and agenda.

Tenets and Assumptions

- Societal oppression is driven by patriarchal structures and other structures that help maintain an imbalance of power.
- Documenting personal experiences is a political move.
- Inclusive approach to fight against patriarchy and related social structure.
- Celebrate the diversity of women and their fights against inequities.

Selected Major Scholars/Schools of Thought

- Betty Friedan (1921–2006)—credited with sparking the second wave of feminism with her book *The Feminine Mystique*; a key figure in women's movement who held various leadership roles in her life, and focused on women's rights, more so than intersections that take her focus away from gender.
- Carol Gilligan (1936–)—feminist, ethics scholar, and psychologist who challenged Lawrence Kohlberg's work on morality where he only studied privileged White men and boys to conclude his opinions on women. Additionally, she critiqued his hierarchical placing of the male view of individual rights and rules than the female's view.
- Simone de Beauvoir (1908–1986)—was known to be an existentialist philosopher, feminist, political activist, and social theorist. One of her famous

texts is *The Second Sex* where she calls for a moral revolution by pointing out that one is not born a woman but becomes one through social construction.

- Patti Lather (birthdate unavailable–)—Lather is a poststructural, feminist qualitative researcher who has contributed to understanding feminist methodology from poststructural perspectives. She has also been a critique of scientifically based research in education, arguing that such discourses have policed and disciplined what can be funded as research and what counts as research, thereby narrowing the understanding of research and ignoring the history of positivism and postpositivism (presented earlier in this unit).

- bell hooks (1952–)—born Gloria Jean Watkins, her pen name being bell hooks, she has focused on the intersectionality of race, class, gender, and connected that intersectionality to social structures of oppression. Through a critical, situated, postmodern (at times) perspective, hooks has discussed key problems in education and in other areas of social science.

- Patricia Bell Scott (birthdate unavailable–)—highly respected feminist scholar who focuses on Black women's narratives, Black women's auto/biographical writing, and gender and development.

- Gloria Anzaldúa (1942–2004)—a Chicana cultural feminist who presented theory in a way that was innovative, accessible, embodied, and experiential; presented her work on mestiza consciousness, shuttling across many borders, and queer theory. Her book *Borderlands/La Frontera: The New Mestiza* is a seminal book that explores her theoretical perspectives, her poems, her ideas for resolution of inner and outer conflicts, grounded in her experiences of growing up on the Mexico–Texas border with unique insights into cultural migration.

- Chandra Mohanty (1955–)—known for her work as a postcolonial and transnational feminist theorist. Her work continuously questions dominant narratives about producing an exotic Other, colonizing effects of dominant narratives, and the ways in which human migration of labor and capital sustain various social structures of oppression.

- Gayatri Spivak Chakravorty (1942–)—her work has been taken up in various fields, especially by poststructural and postmodern feminists. In her seminal work, *Can the Subaltern Speak*, she highlighted the problems of grand narratives created by the dominant group about the Other, where the Other's voice is either absent, minimally present, or distorted. Her self-reflexive translator's introduction for Jacques Derrida's text *De la Grammatologie* was considered path breaking. Her coining of the term "strategic essentialism," where she advocated feminist solidarity for common causes, has been misunderstood and misused, and valued tremendously by various groups of scholars.

Selected Methodologies Used by Feminists

- Critical ethnography
- Critical autoethnography

- Interview studies
- Critical/ethnographic case studies
- Performance ethnography/narratives
- Arts-based and experimental approaches

Selected Critiques of Feminism

- Liberal feminism creates a binary with male and female and excludes male thought and/or men are seen as incapable of being partners with feminists.
- Feminists of color refuse to join White liberal feminists because they do not want to alienate men and want equality for their men and well as themselves.
- Poststructural and postmodern feminism usually deconstructs without any specific ideas for praxis or activism.
- Critical feminists call for emancipation, but notions of emancipation are varied and situated.

Feminism and Your Research Interest: Interactive Exercise

Recall my wiki research focused on the graduate students' learning experiences when working with wiki within the context of a qualitative research class. If I were to conceptualize the inquiry through a feminist focus, I would reframe my research question as the following:

How do female graduate students negotiate the ways in which they collaborate with each other in wikis? In what ways do the female graduate students work with voice and silence while offering feedback in wikis for a qualitative research class?

> The previous set of questions can be justified as questions informed by feminism because they rest on the assumption that there might be some gendered socialization that affects the ways in which women participate in graduate-level classes and offer feedback. The participation of women in these democratically governed webspaces would indicate what discourses the women are drawing upon to inform their roles. Perhaps they were socialized in traditional gender roles. Perhaps they learned to break apart oppressive discourses. Perhaps they were able to develop critical stances to various social systems of oppression early on. Perhaps they are not like the subaltern whose voice cannot be heard. Perhaps they are like the subaltern whose voice cannot be heard. These are various assumptions that are unknown at the onset of the study, and using the abovementioned guiding questions, one can argue that this study can be informed by feminism. However, it would be up to the researcher to identify which kind of feminism she is aligning with.

Now, keeping the abovementioned strategies in mind, what would your research question look like if you informed your research interest through feminism? What kind of feminism appeals to you? Have you aligned your research questions with the tenets of the specific feminism that appeals to you?

Using the tenets of feminism (critique of patriarchy, voice and silence, gendered experiences, existential social structures of oppression connected with patriarchy, women's liberation, equal rights), list how your research question aligns with the tenets.

TABLE 4.5

Tenets of Feminism	Evidence of Tenet in Research Question

Golden Nuggets: Interactive Exercise

In this unit, you have been introduced to various theoretical perspectives and related those perspectives to your research interest. Below I have a couple of activities for you that would help you further crystallize your understanding about theoretical perspectives. In the first activity, you will go back and recall all the research questions you have created and list them in one place. This is so that you can visually have all the questions in the same place and then you can determine which one of the questions speaks best to who you are and what motivates you. That will help you identify your theoretical perspective that you will use for your study.

TABLE 4.6

Theoretical Perspective and Research Question

Research Question Informed by Symbolic Interactionism

Research Question Informed by Phenomenology

Research Question Informed by Hermeneutics

Research Question Informed by Critical Race Theory

Research Question Informed by Feminism

Research Question Informed by Your Own Selected Theory

Can you identify, from the questions in Table 4.6, which one resonates most with you? What theoretical perspective aligns with that question?

The second activity will help generate class discussion. If this activity is not conducted in class, it will still help learners go through the activity for further engagement with theoretical perspectives. This activity is a modified version of an activity that Patti Lather (2006) introduced. She asked the students to think of various objects, people, drinks, etc., as different paradigms and generated discussion around students' choices. Complete the following sentences and provide an explanation:

If **positivism** could be a television show, it would be _____.

Explain below. Remember you are making certain assumptions about the nature of truth, meaning, and the relationship between the observer and observed. This choice needs to be one that would be stable in meaning, and leaves little room for any kind of social construction of meaning. An example (weak one) of positivism as a movie could be any Disney movie where the storyline remains the same, female characters are saved by male characters, good triumphs over evil, and everyone lives happily ever after.

If **interpretivism** could be a television show, it would be _____
_____.

Explain below. Remember you are making certain assumptions about the multiplicities of truths and meanings. This choice could be one that would demonstrate that meaning is constructed, either through a shared experience of a phenomenon, or through making meaning based out of interaction with something symbolic, or making meaning through one's interaction with something textual. An example of interpretivism as a movie could be *Brokeback Mountain* due to the multiple meanings made of the movie.

If **critical theory** could be a television show, it would be _____.

Explain below. Remember you are making certain assumptions about social structures of oppression. This means the show will have to demonstrate the difference between the have's and have not's in some way. There has to be some sort of interrogation of established social structure, some challenge of a dominant narrative, and making room for experiences resulting from some hierarchical ordering of society. An example of critical theory as a movie would be *A Time to Kill*.

If **deconstructivism** could be a television show, it would be_____.

Explain below. Remember you are making certain assumptions about the stability of truth. You have to select some kind of television show where there are structures of truth established and broken apart to never have a stable form of truth or meaning. This means as a viewer you do not walk away with one essential understanding and would look forward to more destabilization of truth and meaning in upcoming episodes. In other words, the show should have elements of deconstruction directly built into its philosophy and execution. An example of a deconstructive movie would be *The Matrix*.

5

UNIT 5: METHODOLOGICAL APPROACHES TO QUALITATIVE INQUIRY

In an earlier unit, you have been briefly oriented to the common types of qualitative research. In this chapter we will explore these options further, while keeping in mind that there are other methodological options that you could explore on your own.

Intentions of This Unit

In this unit, learners will be exposed to certain methodological approaches in qualitative research. Additionally, learners will be able to identify the ways in which these approaches align with other parts of a research project. Learners will also have opportunities to participate in interactive exercises to inform their own research projects.

Methodological Approaches

By now you should be aware of the fact that qualitative research is not only diverse, but there is no one correct way of designing or conducting a qualitative study. Even with the methodological approaches discussed below, there are differences of opinions in terms of how these approaches are taken up by researchers. As you go through the material in this chapter, also remember that often researchers combine approaches together. For example, researchers can conduct a narrative case study, or ethnographic case study, and so on. You are being introduced to basic, foundational understanding. But researchers have blurred boundaries between methodologies to fit their qualitative research projects.

Narrative Inquiry

One of the best descriptions of narrative inquiry I have seen is from Jeong-Hee Kim (personal communications, 2015). She describes narrative inquiry below:

> Narrative inquiry is a storytelling methodology in which a story(ies) of a research participant(s) is researched as a way of knowing. Narrative inquiry has been established in different disciplines including psychology, education, law, medicine, sociology, anthropology, and more, opening the door for the synergy of interdisciplinarity. Using narratives and stories as phenomena to understand what it means to be human, narrative inquiry utilizes inter-disciplinary interpretive lenses with diverse approaches and methods, all revolving around the narratives and stories of research participants. Ety-mologically, narrative means narrate (to tell in Latin) and gnārus (to know in Latin). Hence, narrative inquiry is used as a way of knowing that catches the two sides of narrative, telling as well as knowing.

Narrative inquiry offers a lens, a framework to the study of storied lives. One way to think of narrative inquiry is to think of how participants use stories to interpret their experiences with the world, of a certain event, or the world in general. Therefore, the object of study could be a narrative phenomenon, such as the narrative of patriotism after the 9/11 event in the U.S. or the process of tell-ing stories, or the stories that are told, or the ways in which storied lives become a performance, or reveal identities. Additionally, it is necessary to remember that while narrative somehow implies verbal accounts of stories, stories exist in other spaces too, such as pictures, music, videos, dances, and so on.

Thus, in the most basic form, narrative inquiry is a framework that helps researchers explore, discover, understand, and construct stories based on the participants' recounting of their experiences. Narrative inquiry offers a way to frame how stories are being told and how stories are being reported and what is being selected as stories to be told and remembered. For Clandinin and Con-nelly (2000), narrative inquiry rests on the assumption that human beings like to tell stories and connect socially through stories, and lead storied lives. Therefore, narrative inquiry would be the study of these stories, storied lives, and how par-ticipants come to understand their own story through retelling and interpreting their experiences.

Other understandings of narrative inquiry would be to analyze anything that can be thought of as narrative material (Lieblich, Tuval-Mashiach, & Zilber, 1998). Unlike some other researchers, Lieblich, Tuval-Mashiach, and Zilber (1998) use stories and narratives interchangeably to claim that the stories or narratives as revisited, told, retold, reinterpreted, are part of one's storied life and reveal people's identity.

Types of Narrative Inquiry

While there are many types of narrative inquiry, I discuss six different types of narrative inquiry below. The list is a flexible one, and can be blurred with other types of qualitative methodology and with each other.

Thematic Narratives

These types of narrative inquiry often center around the idea that individuals live storied lives, and by recollecting these stories, they make meaning of their lives. Thus, the stories told are analyzed through an inductive process to identify themes of a storyline and represented as such. For example, see the dissertation works of Leslie Upson (2003) and Leslie Cook (2004).

Biographical Study

These types of study usually involve documenting the narratives of someone else's life. These narratives are usually created through various data sources such as interviews, speeches, documents, writing, pictures, audio, video footage, media records, etc., to create a somewhat comprehensive narrative. For example, see the biography of John F. Kennedy written by Michael O'Brien (2005).

Autoethnography

These are narratives about the self, situated in specific cultural contexts. These narratives reflect on how personal stories are connected to social structures and normative discourses, and the aim often is to document a kind of social history that is otherwise not documented in the way the author is presenting the information. The author is the researcher and the participant simultaneously. Therefore, there is an element of doing the work and observing the self while doing the work. For example, see the works of Laurel Richardson (2013) and Carolyn Ellis (2008).

Life History

These narratives are stories of one's entire life. These are stories that are perhaps not told in history books. Perhaps these stories have a vantage point that requires documentation. While autoethnography or thematic narratives could be around one incident or a few critical incidents, life history narratives span one's entire life. For example, see the work of Denzin (1989).

Oral History

These types of study involve a narrative shared by a person who witnessed a historical event as an insider or an outsider. Conducting oral history research creates room for narratives that might not be present in any documented spaces. Often what oral histories offer is the ways in which people negotiated a historical experience in their everyday lives. For an example of this kind of narrative, see the work of Gardner and Cunningham (1997).

Arts-Based Narratives

These narratives are produced through some artistic formats. Artistic formats can include poems, ethnodrama, documentary, performances, etc. Given that narratives can exist in various spaces, it is important to think of narratives beyond the traditional format of representation. For more examples on these types of work, see Saldaña (2005a), Cahnmann-Taylor (2006), and James Haywood Rolling, Jr. (2011).

Based on the previous discussion, the following can be seen as some of the shared elements in how people think of narrative inquiry.

- Narrative inquiry offers a variety of theoretical frameworks to understand stories.
- Narratives can be understood as phenomena.
- Stories are the ways in which people make meaning of their lives.
- Stories allow for understanding identities.
- Stories can be a performance.
- Stories can exist in many spaces beyond the text.
- The production of stories, the process of storytelling, and retelling is a focus of narrative inquiry.
- What stories are chosen to be shared is a focus of narrative inquiry.
- How stories are structured is a focus of narrative inquiry.

Designing a Narrative Inquiry Study: Using Our Wiki Example

Recall my study of using wikis in my qualitative research classes. In this example, I will walk you through some basic steps of research design, had I used narrative inquiry as my methodological framework. The basic premise of the design is that I would be interested in how the participants' storied their experiences of using wikis in the class and what can be learned from such storied experiences about creating collaborative projects through the use of wikis in graduate-level qualitative research classes.

Research Purpose

The purpose of this study is to explore how students in a graduate-level qualitative inquiry class author their experiences of learning content while collaborating with their peers on wikis for class projects.

Research Questions

1. What are the key stories that participants tell when they describe their experiences of using wikis in graduate-level qualitative research classes?
2. How are such stories being told by the participants? What do the participants choose to highlight in their storytelling?
3. What might be some ways of understanding the experience of using wikis as a collaborative learning tool in graduate-level qualitative research classes as a result of the participants' storytelling?

Research Design (sample selection, duration of study, and data collection methods)

The research design would be narrative inquiry. I would select at least 5 participants for a 6–8-month-long study. If I have more time, say 2–3 years, I would increase the number of participants to 15–20, anticipating my ability to develop an in-depth inquiry and understanding.

The data collection methods would incorporate as many ways in which I could get rich, thick stories. I would include interviews, perhaps some elicited conversations, such as asking participants to show me some of their wiki pages and tell me about the construction of those pages. I might ask the participants to show me some key discussion threads where they made collaborative decisions about what to put on the main wiki page, and tell me about the process. I would use all the webpages, discussion threads, class syllabus, instructional emails, and participants' assignments as data sources. I would also keep a researcher journal to document my thoughts and hunches, build on ideas, and explore subjectivities, and use it as another source of data.

Design a Narrative Inquiry Study: Interactive Exercise

Now it is your turn to design a narrative inquiry study. Think about your research topic and how you might use storied experiences to inform your research topic. Complete the following (use your research journal if you need more space):

Research Purpose

Research Questions (write 2–3 questions aligned with the research purpose)

Research Design (sample selection, duration of study, and data collection methods)

Did this design feel natural or forced based on your sensibilities? Elaborate.

Phenomenological Inquiry

You have already been introduced to phenomenology in an earlier unit, so I invite you to revisit that unit in case you need a refresher. It is important to keep in mind that usually phenomenology provides both a theoretical and methodological framework in qualitative research. What that means is that phenomenology offers a theoretical lens to understand people's lived experiences of a phenomenon. Additionally, phenomenology has specific methodological guidelines that can be used when designing and executing a qualitative study. I guess one can say that the theoretical framework of phenomenology comes with strings attached. The strings in this case would be the methodological guidelines.

The central question asked in phenomenology focuses around the meaning, structure, and essence of the lived experiences of a phenomenon for a person or group of people. Van Maanen (1988, p. 10) states that "phenomenology asks for the very nature of a phenomenon for that which makes a some-'thing' what it is." Husserl (see Ricoeur, 1967) discusses phenomenology as a philosophy. Denzin and Lincoln (2002, 2005) in their various Handbook publications cite phenomenology as an inquiry paradigm, an interpretive theory. Moustakas (1994) uses phenomenology as a research methods framework. Polkinghorne (1989) states that phenomenology explores the structures of consciousness in human experiences.

As you can tell that with such a variation in how people understand and utilize phenomenology, it would again fall on the researcher to demonstrate how s/he understands phenomenology, with whom s/he is aligning theoretical and methodological understandings.

One of the ways to understand phenomenology is how van Maanen (1988) explains:

> From a phenomenological point of view, we are less interested in the factual status of particular instances: whether something happened, how often it tends to happen, or how the occurrence of an experience is related to the prevalence of other conditions and events. For example, phenomenology does not ask, "How do these children learn this particular material?" but it asks, "What is the nature or essence of the experience of learning (so that I can now better understand what this learning experience is like for these children)?" (p. 10)

In other words, van Maanen is teaching us that we are not interested directly in exploring the experience of a particular phenomenon per say but rather the essence of that experience, what lies in the core of the experience, the invariant pattern, if you will. There are some key ideas to keep in mind as you think of utilizing phenomenological approaches in your inquiry.

First, you have to identify a phenomenon. The characteristics of the phenomenon can vary, but there has to be something that situates what you want to study as a phenomenon.

Second, ideally, you would need to work with a group of people who have shared the same phenomenological experience. However, as it often happens in qualitative inquiry, you can also have a phenomenological case study, with few participants (usually 1–5). Again, bear in mind, sample size is not as critical as your ability to develop in-depth theory-driven analysis.

Third, when choosing phenomenology as your methodology, it is important to remember which kind of phenomenology you are aligning with. As demonstrated in an earlier unit, the understanding of phenomenology as a philosophical framework changed once phenomenology was taken up by scholars in the U.S. Therefore, you would need to situate yourself in the broader philosophical discourse of phenomenology as it would have implications for your data collection and data analysis.

Types of Phenomenological Inquiry

While there could be many ways of conducting phenomenological inquiry, we will address three different types of inquiry, transcendental, existential, and hermeneutic. Hermeneutic inquiry and its variant forms of phenomenology is the most commonly used inquiry in qualitative methods.

Transcendental Phenomenology

Transcendental phenomenology is one of the earliest types of phenomenology driven by the works of Husserl (1931) and some of his early assistants after the rise of postpositivism. The focus of transcendental phenomenology is to explore how objects and their meanings are constituted in consciousness. In other words, the focus in transcendental phenomenology is on how knowledge and meaning are constructed, a question of epistemology. Generally, the process of inquiry for this type of phenomenology involves meditative practices where the researcher can retreat within, keep the social discourses of the world outside of conscious awareness, still the mind, focus on what arises from a still space of consciousness, and apply the insights gained to the world when understanding the construction of meaning.

Existential Phenomenology

This kind of phenomenology reflects the evolution of Husserl's earlier thinking through the influence of the works of Heidegger (1962) and Merleau-Ponty (1962) focusing on meaning making through ontology, one's state of being. The key ideas of this kind of phenomenology are grounded in lived experience, modes of being, and ontology. The researcher inquires how we understand our states of being as it shows up in the world around us through our lived experiences.

Hermeneutic Phenomenology

Just as existential phenomenology is an evolved understanding of transcendental phenomenology, hermeneutic phenomenology is an evolved understanding of transcendental and existential phenomenology. This is not to say that this type of phenomenology is superior to the other ones. It is different from the other ones, and you will be drawn to the one that speaks to you personally, if you choose to work with phenomenology. The basic tenets of this kind of phenomenology are interpretation, textual meaning, dialogue, preunderstanding, and tradition. The seminal scholars for this kind of phenomenology are Heidegger (Heidegger, 1982), Gadamer (1989), and Ricoeur (1976) who moved the understanding of phenomenology from descriptive to interpretive, although the boundaries between the two are blurry.

In this type of phenomenology, language, conversations, one's historical context, understanding, and interacting with cultural elements are where the researcher focuses. The assumption is that meanings do not just appear, emerge, or rise, but that through symbolic apparatus of culture, such as religion, art, literature, language, and history, meaning is mediated. At its onset, this kind of phenomenology was used to look at the interpretation of texts with a phenomenological lens emphasizing on language and communication. However, in recent times hermeneutic phenomenology can be expanded to look at other forms of multimedia data.

Based on the previous discussion, the following can be seen as some of the shared elements in how scholars conceptualize phenomenology.

- Most phenomenologists agree that for a study to be phenomenological there has to be some kind of phenomenon that needs to be studied. How this phenomenon is defined varies.
- Phenomenology can be a theoretical and a methodological framework.
- The focus of the study is usually an identification of an essential experience through varied theoretical and philosophical assumptions.
- Transcendental phenomenology focuses on epistemology and how meaning comes into consciousness.
- Existential phenomenology focuses on the nature of reality and state of being, and is also known as ontological phenomenology.
- Hermeneutical phenomenology focuses on the interpretive aspect of meaning making and argues that even in a descriptive account, interpretation is already embedded.

Designing a Phenomenological Study: Using Our Wiki Example

Recall my study of using wikis in my qualitative research classes. In this example, I will walk you through some basic steps of research design, had I used phenomenological inquiry as my methodological framework. The basic premise of the design is that I would be interested in the shared essence(s) of the participants' lived experiences of using wikis in graduate-level qualitative research classes.

Research Purpose

The purpose of this study is to explore how students in graduate-level qualitative research classes explain their shared experiences of using wikis for class projects.

Research Questions

1. How do the participants describe their experiences of using wikis in a graduate-level qualitative research class?
2. What do participants share as challenges when using wikis in a graduate-level qualitative research class?
3. How do participants describe navigating their learning experiences, completing their assignments while using wikis, and any associated challenges?

Research Design (sample selection, duration of study, and data collection methods)

The research design would be a variant of hermeneutic phenomenological inquiry in which I can incorporate multiple types of data. If the duration of the study was 6–8 months, I would include 5–7 participants based on my ability to conduct an in-depth inquiry and deep analysis. If the study were longer, say for 1–2 years, I would increase the number of participants to 10–15 people. The data collection methods would involve multiple interviews per participant (perhaps 3–4), and in-class observations of discussion of collaborative projects for which wikis are used. I might ask participants to show me some of their wiki pages and tell me about the construction of those pages. I might ask the participants to show me some key discussion threads where they made collaborative decisions about what to put on the main wiki page, and tell me about the process. I would use all the webpages, discussion threads, class syllabus, instructional emails, and participants' assignments as data sources. I would also keep a researcher journal to document my thoughts and hunches, build on ideas, and explore subjectivities, and use it as another source of data.

Design a Phenomenological Study: Interactive Exercise

Now it is your turn to design a phenomenological study. Think about your research topic and how you might use lived experiences of a phenomenon to inform your research topic. Complete the following (use your research journal if you need more space):

Research Purpose

Research Questions (write 2–3 questions aligned with the research purpose)

Research Design (sample selection, duration of study, and data collection methods)

Did this design feel natural or forced based on your sensibilities? Elaborate.

Grounded Theory

Similar to other methodological approaches, grounded theory too has been adopted and adapted in various ways by qualitative researchers. Additionally, some people use grounded theory as a methodology, while others use grounded theory methods to inform their work. The former group uses grounded theory as a blueprint for guiding their work and constructs a theory grounded in their data, whereas the latter uses grounded theory methods as data management and analysis tools instead of informing their entire blueprint of research.

Grounded theory has gone through many adoptions and adaptations since its initial conceptualization by Barney Glaser and Anselm Strauss (1967/2009). Since then Glaser (1992) and Strauss and Corbin (1998) have disagreed and branched off with their own schools of thought. Later, Kathy Charmaz (2002; 2006) introduced and popularized constructivist grounded theory, which created more divisions within the field with researchers using grounded theory methodology in divergent ways to suit their research agendas. I will discuss two broad ways in which the grounded theory differs, which is the classical or objectivist grounded theory, and the second-generation grounded theory that is informed by Charmaz's (2002) work, as constructivist grounded theory.

In the most rudimentary terms, grounded theory methodology attempts to discover theory grounded in the analysis of data collected during qualitative research. This is because several grounded theory scholars believe that sometimes a priori theories are not the best-suited theories to understand participants' conceptualization and meaning making of their experiences. Therefore, they suggest that theories should be developed from data collected after thorough analysis of various data sources that reflect the participants' experiences, actions, and interactions in social situations. The analysis of data collected in grounded theory is inductive, and not deductive, with the assumption that the theory generated will be intimately connected and grounded to the data collected and analyzed. Typically, grounded theory methodologies are suitable approaches when there is little known about a subject so that a thorough investigation can be conducted to generate a theory grounded in data.

Types of Grounded Theory Inquiry

Classical/objectivist grounded theory is ontologically positivist or postpositivist, while constructivist grounded theory is relativist.

Classical/Objectivist Grounded Theory

The goal of the classical/objectivist grounded theory method is to offer a well-developed, well-defended rationale for theory generated and developed during a study. The theories generated from conducting traditional grounded theory work are mid-level theories, which are abstractions of social phenomena and processes collected during the research. Typically, classical grounded theorists focused on one main concern and its continual resolution, which is also known as the core category. The researcher tries to claim a value neutral, dispassionate role, separate from the research participants, and sees the world, data, as an investigator or outside expert, and does not analyze the possibilities emerging out of the relationship between the researcher and the participants.

While Glaser and Strauss went their separate ways, Glaser did not identify any philosophical influence on grounded theory methods, whereas Strauss and Corbin (1998) identified pragmatism and symbolic interactionism as the influential philosophy for grounded theory. These traditional grounded theorists believe that there is a tangible reality but that it is only imperfectly perceived. Through saturating categories and developing conceptual theories, classical grounded theorists leave open the possibility that a theory can be changed if new information is identified. The conceptual theory generation, ideally, should transfer and be applicable to other situations.

Constructivist Grounded Theory

Constructivist grounded theory is ontologically relativist, and epistemologically subjectivist. Constructivist grounded theory situates the researcher and the participant in an interpretive exchange where neither enters the research space without the influence of the world, their individual histories, beliefs, assumptions, informing the meanings they make of each other, their experiences outside and within the research space. Unlike classical grounded theory, constructivist grounded theory does not center upon a core category and makes room for multiple truths and perceptions, instead of focusing on one main concern.

Charmaz (2006) advocates for developing "provisionally true" and "verifiable theory of reality" (p. 273) for constructivist grounded theory methodology. This approach is in contrast to the premise of classical grounded theory where the focus is on presenting plausible hypotheses and generating concepts. The assumption is that if done correctly, in a classical grounded theory study, the concept will still be stable even if the people have varied perceptions. Constructivist grounded theorists see data collection and analysis as a shared experience between the participants and the researcher. Constructivist studies examine how participants form meanings and actions, and get as close to the experience as possible. The data analysis conducted by constructivist grounded theorists could be referred to as "data forming" since the researcher is interacting with the participant during the data collection and analysis process. The goal is to uncover values, beliefs, and assumptions of the researcher and the participants than to have specific prescriptive methods.

Charmaz (2006) also advocates for developing theoretical categories and then saturating the categories. Through these processes, Charmaz (2006) suggests conceptualizing a theory through diagramming, sorting through, and integrating information so that the theory will be grounded in data collected and analyzed. However, Charmaz (2006) does present guidelines for some processes in which researchers can engage when conducting this kind of work. These guidelines include various approaches to coding, verifying understanding, documenting researcher thoughts through memoing, journaling, and annotating notes. She discusses ways in which rich data could be gathered, managed through line-by-line coding, focused coding, axial coding, and theoretical coding. She advocates for memo writing, where memos are space holders for documenting the researcher's thoughts, negotiations, interpretations, hunches, and so on.

Based on the previous discussion, the following can be seen as some of the shared or essential elements in grounded theory studies:

- Grounded theory can be taken up as a methodology or a set of methodological tools.
- Glaser denied philosophical influence on grounded theory, whereas Strauss emphasized the influence of pragmatism and symbolic interactionism.
- Kathy Charmaz popularized constructivist grounded theory informed by social constructivism and situated grounded theory in the interpretive realm of qualitative research.
- All variations of grounded theory focus on some form of theory development.
- All variations of grounded theory advocate for some form of initial coding and categorization of data.
- Many grounded theorists use memo writing as a way to document process, record thoughts, identify hunches, and write reminders to self.
- Theoretical sampling is a key process of grounded theory research where the researcher expands on the sampling based on new information gained during data collection and analysis.
- Many grounded theory researchers engage in constant comparative analysis so that they can ensure they are working through all parts of the data collected and relating them.
- After initial coding, there exists some form of intermediate coding before theoretical concept(s) are finalized.
- Identifying a core category is relevant to many grounded theory researchers, especially those who are aligned with classical grounded theory.
- All variations of grounded theory advocate some form of inductive construction of abstract categories.

Designing a Constructivist Grounded Theory Study: Using Our Wiki Example

Recall my study of using wikis in my qualitative research classes. In this example, I will walk you through some basic steps of research design, had I used grounded theory as my methodological framework. The basic premise of the design is that

I would be interested in the ways in which participants formed meanings about using wikis in my qualitative research class, with the intent to theorize that meaning-making process.

Research Purpose

The purpose of this study is to explore how students in graduate-level qualitative research classes constructed meanings about their experiences of using wikis integrated into a class project.

Research Questions

1. How do the participants describe their experiences of using wikis in a graduate-level qualitative research class?
2. What ways do the participants construct meaning about their interactions with their peers while conducting their projects using wikis?
3. How do participants describe their meaning making of the content in the class while using wikis for a class project?

Research Design (sample selection, duration of study, and data collection methods)

The research design would involve a maximum variation sampling. This means I would start by selecting a sample size of students who could give me as varied a perspective as I could obtain. So I might select 10 students. But after talking to them, I might realize that I need to talk to some students who were distance education students and some who were single-parent students as their perspectives might shed new light that I did not consider. So the sampling size would increase until I have included as many varying perspectives as I can. This kind of maximum variation in sampling also leads to a saturation point where information from the participants would not offer any more insights, and would be a repeat of what others have said before. I would consider a 4–6-month period of data collection and another 4–6 months for data analysis. Data collection methods could include interviews, elicited interviews, class observation notes, wiki participation, assignments, and information in the wiki discussion threads. I would also keep a researcher journal to document my thoughts and hunches, build on ideas, and explore subjectivities, and use it as another source of data in addition to analytical memos. In an analytical memo, the researcher makes a "note to self" to follow up on hunches, look up literature, or elaborate a thought, interrogate data, develop a conclusion, or connect another part of the data, or anything else that the researcher deems relevant in order to connect with the data while being grounded in the purpose of the research.

Design a Grounded Theory Study: Interactive Exercise

Now it is your turn to design a phenomenological study. Think about your research topic and how you might use lived experiences of a phenomenon to inform your research topic. Complete the following (use your research journal if you need more space):

Research Purpose

Research Questions (write 2–3 questions aligned with the research purpose)

Research Design (sample selection, duration of study, and data collection methods)

Did this design feel natural or forced based on your sensibilities? Elaborate.

Case Study

Case study research is commonly used in qualitative research to answer focused questions with in-depth inquiries. Case studies can be done for relatively short periods of time, ranging from a few weeks, months, to a whole year. Usually case studies investigate issues that are occurring during the time of the research, unlike biographical or historical research. Case studies are also targeted at information-rich sources for in-depth understanding and can also be used to inform policies or to uncover contributing reasons for cause-and-effect relationships.

As you must have guessed by now, there are multiple definitions of case studies research. For example, "Case studies are reports of alternative paradigm inquiries" (Lincoln & Guba, 2002, p. 213), yet the case study "does not implicate any particular approach" (Wolcott, 1992, p. 36). Yin defines case study as an "empirical inquiry that investigates a contemporary phenomenon within its real-life context, especially when the boundaries between phenomenon and context are not clearly evident" (Yin, 1994, p. 13).

While Wolcott defines case study as an end-product of research, Merriam asserts that a "qualitative case study is an intensive, holistic description and analysis of a single instance, phenomenon, or social unit" (Merriam, 1998, p. 21). Merriam adds to her understanding of case studies by stating, "I have concluded that the single most defining characteristic of case study research lies in delimiting the object of study, the case" (Merriam, 1998, p. 27).

Though Merriam advocates for a boundary or identification of the scope of a study, she acknowledges that there is freedom in what might be conceptualized as a case. A case may involve studying a person, program, policy, or any other phenomenon that is intrinsically bounded by the interest of the researcher (Merriam, 1998). Furthermore, Merriam (1998, p. 13) states that case studies can be responsible for discovering "new relationships, concepts, and understandings" inductively rather than deductively.

Adding to two other researchers' understanding of case studies, Bromley (1986) states that the purpose of a case study is "not to find the 'correct' or 'true' interpretation of the facts, but rather to eliminate erroneous conclusions so that one is left with the best possible, the most compelling, interpretation" (p. 38). Hamel and colleagues (Hamel, Dufour, & Fortin, 1993) posit that the case study "has proven to be in complete harmony with the three words that characterize any qualitative method: describing, understanding and explaining" (p. 5).

And in my own work (Bhattacharya, 2009b), I have argued that theoretical influences inform how one conceptualizes case study research. From that perspective, I have become critical of the concept of holistic understanding in case study research, or in any form of qualitative research for that matter. This is because no matter how much we try, we are not able to capture the whole. At best, we are documenting what we are able to understand, gather, interpret, analyze, in the moments of time we have shared with the participant and are invested in reporting the results of our inquiry. Our understanding changes over time, which implies that so does the understanding of the participants of their own lives.

Types of Case Study Inquiries

Based on the intent of case study research, case study research can be understood broadly in three different ways. However, I would caution to not hold the types as stable categorizations that cannot be blurred. One of the most important aspects of case study research is what one considers to be a case. A case is a bounded system and it is up to the researcher to create the boundary of what a case ought to be with justification from existing literature and theoretical perspectives. The three broad types of case studies are single instrumental case study, collective/ multiple case study, and intrinsic case study. Case studies can also include numbers in them (as could many other types of qualitative inquiry), as long as they add insight to the case being studied. Numerical information could be a data source and is often integrated in the final representation of results.

Single Instrumental Case Study

This kind of case study focuses on a unique, information-rich situation, concern, or problem and selects a bounded system as a case to study this case. The bounded system in this instance could include one participant, many participants, or an entire organization. The scope of the research is driven by how the researcher operationalizes the bounded system informed by the concern/problem that s/he is interested in investigating. For more on this type of case study research, see Stake (1995).

Collective/Multiple Case Studies

In this type of case study research, the researcher selects an issue or problem to investigate, defines what the bounded system of a case would look like, and selects several cases to explore the issue. Here too, a case could include one person, multiple people, or a whole organization. Selected cases are representative of the issue under investigation and information-rich sources. Reports in this type of inquiries include a report on individual cases and a cross-case report too. This way the researcher is able to provide analytical insights on things that are similar and different between the two cases. For more on this type of case study research, see Yin (2003).

Intrinsic Case Study

This kind of case study is different from the previous types described as the focus here is the case itself, whereas the other types focused on an issue and identified representative bounded systems that were defined as cases. Here a case could be a student of color in an all-White class, and her experiences in formal and informal academic spaces or a program which has a high record of success for helping students of color in middle school in a southern U.S. town engaged in science and mathematics. For more on this type of case study research, see Stake (1995).

Based on the previous discussion, the following can be seen as some of the shared elements in how people think of case studies.

- It is important to have a strong understanding and justification for how one defines a bounded system to be a case.
- A case could be a person, persons, or a whole organization.
- Theoretical perspectives, and by extension epistemologies, inform how one approaches case study work.
- Case studies focus on a specific contemporary issue instead of the work done in biographical or historical studies.
- Case study can be a methodology or a form of representation.
- Numerical information can be part of case study research (or other types of qualitative inquiry).

Example of a Multiple Case Study

I will use my dissertation study as an example for this section. I was exploring the experiences of two female graduate students from India in higher education in the U.S. in their first year of being in a foreign country. I was interested in looking at their navigation in various spaces and how being an international student in a system different to their own revealed things that stood out to the participants.

Research Purpose

The purpose of this study is to examine how two female Indian graduate students who have been in the U.S. for no more than 1.0 year negotiate their initial experiences while pursuing their education.

Research Questions

1. What expectations do the two female Indian graduate students retain from their Indian upbringing? What expectations do they discard or modify? How do female Indian graduate students conceptualize their modification of expectations?
2. How do the two female Indian graduate students conceptualize their academic experiences (e.g. classroom experiences, relationships with advisors, expectations for performance, understanding of their role as graduate assistants, and interaction with other students and people of diverse backgrounds, etc.)?

Research Design

I conducted informal conversations, semistructured open-ended in-depth interviews, photo- and object-elicited conversations, and participant observations. I also kept a researcher journal during the 8-month-long study.

Data Analysis

Generally speaking, data analysis in case studies are inductive in nature where the researcher examines raw data sources, chunks information from those raw data sources, groups information that is similar in meaning, and then looks for commonalities across and within these groups to identify broad patterns or themes. We will discuss this process in detail in a later unit.

Researchers sometimes use the constant comparative method for analyzing information in case studies. Merriam (1998) states, "The constant comparative

TABLE 5.1 Sample Cross-Case Comparison

Spaces	Neerada	Yamini
Formal academia	Respected advisor even when she did not feel supported. Practiced acts of resistance and accommodation strategically.	Supported by advisor. Did not connect with non-Indian professors beyond classroom requirements.
Career fairs and networking	No comparable experience.	Became comfortable with forced social conversations toward the end of the program after feeling alienated. Marginalized by other NRIs due to her lack of experience and time in the U.S.
Informal academia	Was not as successful in developing a community of support, although made efforts toward the end to build bridges. She was informed that there was a racial divide in the department.	Developed a community of support with mostly international and some domestic White students. Perceived cultural alienation from some White students in the department. Certain conversations enhanced her sense of Indian-ness.
Hickory Towers	Participated in community activities only to find that the levels of expectation were beyond her means to meet. Accepted marginalization	Did not feel the need to participate in that community. Emphasized that being Indian did not mean that they would be an automatic community.

Spaces	Neerada	Yamini
	even at the cost of loneliness. Different expectations about being an extension of college life from India.	Marginal membership to which she was indifferent. Became preferential to more traditional Indian food, clothes, and entertainment.
Alternate communities of support	Found the same alternate community as Yamini and mentioned that she thought that she could really be herself in this community without the gazes she perceived existed in Hickory Towers.	Used an alternate group of female Indian friends as a community of support who lived in on-campus graduate student apartments.
Family visit/ memories of India	Family memories and conversations became a way for Neerada to stay grounded in her experiences in India.	Family visit reflected gendered and class-based expectations. Yamini desired her independence at the cost of her familiar privileges.
Nonresident Indian (NRI) in the U.S.	Experienced the need to become more traditional and religious than she was in India. Disliked distorted cultural practices.	Yamini grappled with this issue when she was forced to think of her NRI status by the recruiters. From previous exposure Yamini experienced the need to emulate NRI life of compromised privileges.

method involves comparing one segment of data with another to determine similarities and differences. Data are grouped together on a similar dimension. This dimension is tentatively given a name; it then becomes a category. The overall object of this analysis is to seek patterns in the data" (p. 18). However, it is not necessary that everyone takes up this approach to analyzing data.

I looked at how the participants' experiences differed based on the spaces in which the experiences occurred. I presented a cross-comparison chart to demonstrate analytic insights from the study.

Design a Case Study: Interactive Exercise

Now it is your turn to design a case study. Think about your research topic and how you might use information-rich cases to inform your research topic. Complete the following (use your research journal if you need more space):

Research Purpose

Research Questions (write 2–3 questions aligned with the research purpose)

Research Design (sample selection, duration of study, and data collection methods)

Did this design feel natural or forced based on your sensibilities? Elaborate.

Ethnography

Ethnography is the study of culture grounded historically in anthropology but currently has been taken up in various fields. However, culture is not that easy of a term to define as we have discussed in an earlier section. Goodenough (1973) frames culture as something human beings learn together, reflected in the form of beliefs, values, rituals, customs, recipes, rules, public values, and systems of customs. Culture then can be something that is taught to and learned by the members who belong to the group. With this understanding of culture, culture can be broadly thought of as a nation and narrowly thought of as being fans of a football team. Preissle and Grant (2004) tell us the following:

> Classical model of ethnography was developed primarily by anthropologists to document ways of life around the world presumed to be changing rapidly under the pressures of colonization and Westernization (Boas, 1940; Malinowski, 1922). Researchers took a visible role in a community or culture for an extended period of time and wrote a contextualized account attempting to portray the culture from the perspectives of its participants. (p. 164)

Ethnography can also indicate methodological procedures as well as a form of representation of data. This is similar to case study where case study could also be a methodology and a form of representation. Additionally, like grounded theory, people often use ethnographic methods for their studies without actually doing an ethnography as many scholars might not have access, time, or resources to conduct an ethnography.

Wolcott (1995) explains ethnography as "a picture of the 'way of life' of some identifiable group of people" (p. 188). It is a way to paint a picture of the world in which the participants live and learn and perform culture. Spradley (1979) describes conducting ethnography as a cultural experience for the researcher, as the researcher has to immerse herself in the culture that she wishes to study. Therefore, the researcher is "embedded in and ultimately concerned with cultural description" (Wolcott, 1980, p. 58). This means that conducting an ethnographic study has to be done with the focus being on deep understanding of human behavior grounded in some cultural context. This kind of work requires "a specialized form of fieldwork, in which culture is a central concept, where deep engagement over time with a culture is expected, and where a central goal is the presentation of an insider's view of that culture" (Preissle & Grant, 2004, p. 165).

Therefore, ethnography is an interpretive description that the researcher provides in order to present the participants' understanding of their culture, to whatever extent that is possible. It would be inaccurate to claim that such a description or interpretation is value neutral and does not reflect the researcher's subjectivities. Like any other qualitative methodology, ethnography can be informed by various theoretical frameworks. Thus, a qualitative researcher can conduct ethnography using an interpretive theory, such as symbolic interactionism (Geertz, 1973; Lamb, 2000), or critical theory (Ladson-Billings, 2009; Madison, 2005), or postmodernism, or postmodern feminism (Visweswaran, 1994; Wolf, 1992).

This is also a good time to discuss insider/outsider research. In the past, Margaret Mead and Clifford Geertz studied groups to whom they were cultural outsiders. There were cautions of not getting so close to the culture one studies where the person goes native and becomes more of a cultural insider than an outsider. However, this argument has been debated by scholars of color across the world. Linda Tuhiwai Smith, a Maori scholar, demonstrated clearly when cultural outsiders from a dominant group chose to study a culture about which they had no real understanding and could not understand from their subjective positions that they had done damage and produced oppressive, incorrect, and dehumanizing accounts of cultures they had studied (Smith, 1999/2012). Thus, many communities prefer insiders to conduct research about the communities instead of outsiders producing accounts that lead to further oppression. There are several examples of insiders conducting research in their own communities dating back to the early 19th century with the works of W.E.B. Dubois (1899) who studied his own Black community in Philadelphia. Zora Neale Hurston (1935) conducted anthropological studies in Black communities, and Kamala Visweswaran (1994) conducted ethnographic work in India as a member of the community that she studied.

Ethnographers usually collect data for at least a year and a half to claim deep, rich understanding of a culture. There are ethnographers who have spent at least 10 years in the field to collect data. Field, in this case, does not mean the place where grass grows. Field refers to the research site or sites within which an ethnographer can engage with a certain culture. Sample size is not relevant for ethnography, as this is a study of culture. Therefore, what is relevant is time spent within the cultural context that is being studied.

One of the characteristics of ethnography that is key is that the group or culture being studied should have been together or intact for a long period of time so that cultural values are shared by members and so that an outsider can study these values and talk to the members and understand the ways in which the participants experience and describe their membership in the group.

You need to become familiar with emic and etic perspectives in ethnography. Emic perspectives refer to the perspectives of cultural insiders, and etic refers to the perspectives of cultural outsiders. The more a researcher can obtain, understand, and internalize an emic perspective, the more the researcher will be able to describe cultural experiences from the participants' perspectives. However, an etic perspective allows the researcher to add insights from an outsider that might not be possible from an insider position. Even when a researcher is a cultural insider, the researcher still shifts between being an insider and outsider because the researcher position requires public documentation of something that is shared only between the group members. The researcher position implies a gaze on a group of people, which automatically puts the researcher in an outsider position. Thus, qualitative researchers often outline how their positions in the research influenced data collection, analysis, and interpretation, in addition to ethical cross-roads they might have encountered.

Types of Ethnographic Research

As with other methodologies presented thus far, there are many ways to conduct an ethnography and it is not possible to list them all in this book. I am presenting an abbreviated list of the types of ethnographies and their associated descriptions.

Realist Ethnography

This is the approach of ethnographies that early researchers used which is mostly informed through an interpretive perspective. Therefore, the purpose of these types of ethnographies was to gain a descriptive understanding of a culture to which the researcher was an outsider. These types of ethnographies are those where the researcher attempted to remain value neutral and wrote in third person with the assumption that there was an object to be observed (in this case, people and their cultural behaviors), and with the right process, these accounts should be objective accounts, something that any researcher could observe and document should they choose to do such a thing. The ethnographer's subjectivities were not discussed as if the ethnographer was the man behind the curtain offering facts for consumption. The ethnographer interviews the participants and presents their words in direct quotes and offers the ultimate interpretation of the quotes, as the voice of authority. For more on realist ethnographies, see the work of van Maanen (1988).

Critical Ethnography

This kind of ethnography is driven by the assumption that our society is divided hierarchically, and deep ethnographic research can interrogate the various ways inequities in our society are sustained and promoted. Inequities can be viewed through different lenses such as race, ethnicity, economic status, gender, national origin, sexuality, disability, socioeconomic status, language, and others as well as the intersectionality of these. The axes of social difference—disability/ableism, gender/sexism, age/ageism, sexuality/heterosexism, race/racism, and the intersectionalities of oppression, power, and privilege could also be a way to understand how inequities function in people's lived experiences in certain cultural groups. Thus, a critical ethnography would provide descriptive and interpretive accounts of how such inequities create certain lived experiences for a group of people. The researchers who conduct critical ethnographies do not claim to be value neutral or assume that what they provide as their account is objective. They value the relationship built with the participant and put themselves under the same ethnographic gaze as the one under which the participants are placed in such studies. For more on critical ethnographies, see the works of Carspecken and Apple (1992) and D. Soyini Madison (2005).

Virtual Ethnography

This type of ethnography is also known as online ethnography, or netnography. Simply put, researchers who conduct virtual ethnography are attempting to study the culture of certain online communities. These communities could exist in discussion boards, chatrooms, virtual environments, or in certain websites where users interact with each other. Researchers could use many ethnographic methods such as interviewing, using technologies such as Skype, Google Hangout, and FaceTime. Some researchers also use synchronized chat to conduct interviews; however, in such interviews, information about nonverbal communication is not captured well because even on Skype or Google Hangout, the researcher is limited in what she can observe within the frame of the screen. Another issue associated with virtual ethnography is the question of how the researcher would obtain multiple sources of information from a participant, if all she knows is someone's chatroom ID. Thus, depending on one's theoretical and methodological framework, issues of verifiability could be compromised. In my own work (2013), while guiding students to conduct virtual ethnographies, I suggested that students ask questions of the participants that are relevant to the participants' experiences in the online spaces only and not about spaces where the researcher does not have any access. Additionally, I recommended that one's understanding of truth needs to be situated, and at any rate, qualitative researchers are not always in a position to claim knowledge of absolute truth. Thus, working in this space means asking questions about cultural understandings which can be inquired through the information present in the online communities that are being studied. For more on virtual ethnographies, see the works of Boellstorff, Nardi, Pearce, and Taylor (2012) and Hine (2000).

Digital Ethnography

Digital ethnography is a form of ethnography that is conducted in various digital spaces. In other words, the understanding of culture and cultural contexts are derived from the "field" which consists of digital sources of information, such as text, video or images, and social media, that depict some form of social relations between groups, within groups, between nations, within nations, or whatever way the researcher conceptualizes the scope of the study. A digital ethnographer might be interested in exploring the cultural beliefs of a subgroup in Facebook, or a breast cancer support group in a discussion forum, or look at the cultural narratives formed based around women of color winning beauty pageants in the U.S. The researcher can determine what would comprise the various field sites while conducting digital ethnography.

When a traditional ethnographer goes into the field, she takes with her some recording device to document interviews and observations. A digital ethnographer uses a different set of tools such as screen-capture software, archiving tools for web-based information, servers for storage of large files, blogs for reflections and interactions with participants where relevant, and software to help manage the volume of content. Thus, the biggest difference between traditional and digital ethnography is where the two inquiries are conducted. For more on digital ethnography, see the works of Underberg and Zorn (2013) and Horst and Miller (2012).

Visual Ethnography

Visual ethnography refers to the practice of conducting ethnographic research which is strongly driven by photographs, videos, and other visual materials to obtain cultural understandings. Ethnographic studies involve the researcher being "there" in the field, bearing witness to the society or culture studied. Visual ethnography is still a form of ethnography, i.e., bearing witness to the society or culture studied, but the investigation is strongly focused on cultural objects, artifacts that are already prominent visual representations with their own meanings for the cultural insiders. Like any other form of ethnography, visual ethnography can also be realist, interpretive, critical, or even deconstructive. The theoretical alignment will drive the cultural meanings made and representations put forward as findings of a visual ethnographic study. Visual ethnographies do not exclude other ethnographic methods such as interviews or observations, but have a strong focus on visual methods, collection of visual data, and analysis of visual artifacts that are meaningful to the culture studied. For more on visual ethnography, see the works of Sarah Pink (2001a, 2001b), Gillian Rose (2001/2012), Howard Becker (2002), Marcus Banks (2001), and Nicholas Mirzoeff (2002/2012).

Based on the previous discussion, the following can be seen as some of the shared elements in how people think of ethnographies.

- Ethnographies involve understanding a culture, bearing witness to a selected social group.
- Culture need not be limited to people of different ethnic backgrounds as many social groups have their own cultures.
- Ethnographies imply a prolonged duration in the field extending well over a year.
- Many people use ethnographic methods without engaging in a full ethnography.

- There are various theoretical, epistemic, and ontological drives that influence the type of inquiry conducted and the ways in which data interpretation occurs in ethnographic research.
- Ethnographic research can be conducted through realist, interpretive, critical, and deconstructive theoretical approaches.
- There are moves to incorporate the digital landscape and tools available in the digital landscape into the cannon of ethnography.
- Visual ethnographies are more than incorporating visual elements in an ethnography. It is the ethnographic analysis of cultural artifacts that are visual in addition to the ethnographic analysis of visual sources of data.

Considerations for Ethnography

If you choose to do an ethnographic study, you have to ask yourself the following questions:

- Can you gain entry to the culture you want to study?
- Are you an insider or outsider to the culture? How will you negotiate your role in the culture?
- Are you approaching your data collection process guided by your theoretical framework?
- Have you considered the time frame of this research and what you need to do after you leave the field?
- Have you considered whether you would need to have access to a key informant for the culture in which you plan to immerse yourself?
- Have you investigated the basic cultural protocols so that, even as an outsider when you first start the study, you do not break protocols in a way that costs your membership in the culture?

Often researchers don't have the **time** required to conduct a full-blown ethnography. In those instances, they remain in the field for 4–6 months and claim that they have conducted **an interpretive study using ethnographic methods.** Conducting a study for a shorter period of time can still allow for an in-depth understanding, but not the kind of in-depth cultural understanding that comes from a prolonged engagement.

Example of a Mini Virtual Ethnography Study

I have introduced students to virtual ethnography by using a virtual multiuser 3-D environment called Second Life. We collect data from Second Life, a three-dimensional, multiuser, online, object-based, virtual environment where users from all over the world log in and create their own cultural experiences. I called it mini virtual ethnography because the period of engagement in the culture was for only 4 months. Analysis of data is only preliminary and not a comprehensive attempt.

Research Purpose

The purpose of this study is to understand cultural attachments of users in certain groups in Second Life.

Research Questions

1. What are the participants' experiences of being part of a cultural group in Second Life?
2. How do participants describe their attachments to their cultural group in Second Life?
3. What inspires participants to remain a member in their cultural group in Second Life?

Research Design

The researcher studied members who belonged to a cultural group called International Society for Technology in Education (ISTE). ISTE had an island in Second Life to complement their offline presence. They conduct several chats, conferences, and networking opportunities among educators who are interested in technology integration. The researcher stayed in the environment for 4 months, conducted several interviews over text and voice, verified understanding with the participants, conducted participant observations, took photographs of the cultural site to conduct visual analysis via screenshots, and collected relevant cultural artifacts from the cultural site.

Data Analysis Process for a Mini Virtual Ethnography

Data analysis was inductive, and therefore similar in nature to what was described as the data analysis process for case study, except in ethnography the focus is not on a case but on the culture. Therefore, several ethnographers code, categorize, and identify cultural themes that are evident across and within all data sources. Below is an example of an outline of the preliminary analysis of a mini ethnographic study of the culture of ISTE in Second Life.

The cultural themes were identified after analyzing interview transcripts, observations, snapshots of various cultural events, space, people, web pages, and other relevant archived documents. The Roman numbered bolded statements are cultural themes. The lettered bullet points represent categories. The numerical listing of words and phrases are some examples of codes, although not an exhaustive list of codes identified in the study.

I. Assisting newbies in becoming accustomed to Second Life is a focus of ISTE Island.

    A. Welcoming and accommodating

        1. Anything I can help with, just ask
        2. Let me help you a bit
        3. Let me offer you friendship

    B. Advice given to newbies

        1. Do not trust people asking for money
        2. Be careful of information you share
        3. People more prone to interact if not new looking

II. Informing newbies about Second Life is a purpose of the culture on ISTE Island.

    A. Description of Second Life

        1. Global society
        2. Business structure similar to real life
        3. Place for expression

    B. Economic structure in Second Life

        1. Goods and services
        2. Currency and foreign exchange
        3. Individual ventures and businesses

    C. Reasons for participating in Second Life

        1. Technology is incredible
        2. Networking and exploring

The above was an extremely abbreviated description of ethnography. For more details in using Second Life as a space for virtual ethnography, you can read my chapter on this topic (Bhattacharya, 2013).

Design an Ethnography: Interactive Exercise

Now it is your turn to design an ethnography. Think about your research topic and how you might use cultural experiences to inform your research topic. Complete the following (use your research journal if you need more space):

Research Purpose

Research Questions (write 2–3 questions aligned with the research purpose)

Research Design (sample selection, duration of study, and data collection methods)

Did this design feel natural or forced based on your sensibilities? Elaborate.

Golden Nuggets: Interactive Exercise

Reflecting on what you have been presented in this unit, consider which methodological approach would be most appropriate for your research interest. In order to help you, I have prompted you with some questions. Some of these questions have been presented to you before. In this unit, you can reflect on them again based on your sharper understanding of methodological approaches. If your answers are similar to before, then you can crystallize your ideas further. If your answers are different from what you said before, then you have some reflection to do.

1. What is the purpose of your study? Are you trying to understand, interrogate, or deconstruct?

2. Which one of the methodological approaches presented here do you think is appropriate for your study? What do you think you will be able to gain using this approach?

3. In what ways are you thinking that your research purpose, theoretical framework, and methodology are aligned?

4. Do you see yourself combining any of these approaches? If so, what aspects of the different approaches can you see combining? What will you be able to do if you combine approaches or elements of these approaches?

5. What do you need to know more in order to sharpen your understanding of your research (design, methodology, theoretical framework, something else)?

6

UNIT 6: DATA COLLECTION METHODS

In this unit, we will learn specifically about three main types of data collection methods. As with all the previous units, every aspect of qualitative research presented in this book can be expanded further as its own text because of the diversity and depth of information in the field.

Intentions of This Unit

In this unit, learners will be exposed to three different types of data collection methods in qualitative research, namely conducting interviews, making observations, and collecting relevant documents. Learners will be able to participate in some interactive activities to enhance their understanding of data collection methods in qualitative inquiry.

What Are Qualitative Interviews?

Generally speaking, qualitative interviews are conversations between the interviewer and the interviewee. Depending on the researcher's positionality, these conversations take different forms. Do not mistake conversations to mean that anyone, without training or practice, can conduct qualitative interviews. Qualitative interviews are intentional, with specific ways of inquiring, with reflexivity, among other things that are only improved with practice. If done well, it appears to be deceptively easy.

There are many ways qualitative researchers use conversations as a way of understanding an experience. These ways include but are not limited to:

- formal semistructured interview
- in-depth open-ended interview

- informal open-ended interview
- natural conversations.

Formal semistructured interviews involve the researcher preparing questions in advance with possible probes identified. The researcher usually sticks to the prepared protocol while making room for unexpected directions in the interview if it occurs and is relevant to the study. The researcher does so to maintain consistency across interviews and to compare responses for each question for the participants in the study.

In-depth open-ended interviews usually focus on digging deep into one's experiences with a few key questions prepared in advance. The researcher focuses on using the key questions as probes to peel away a superficial understanding of one's experiences to a deeper understanding of one's experiences.

Informal open-ended interviews usually involve the researcher and the participant having a casual conversation about the participant's experiences in an informal manner. In other words, the researcher usually identifies key areas that she would like to touch on during the interview but does not necessarily come to the interview with a set of structured questions. The feel of the interview is informal where the researcher guides the participant through insightful probes that create a conversation between the two of them. Even though the interview could feel informal in its tone, the researcher is quite mindful in setting up the conversation this way and uses broad probing questions periodically to move the conversation forward.

Natural conversations usually involve an equal exchange between the researcher and the participant. To an outsider, it would appear two people are having a conversation with a natural flow of talk between the two of them. In this type of conversation, the interviewee gets to ask the researcher questions that she deems relevant or necessary. Information exchange is bidirectional.

What I advise my students is to forget the labels surrounding interviews and discover what feels natural for them while conducting interviews. If what feels natural is a combination of the four types listed above, then so be it. What is critical is that you, as an interviewer, have to feel comfortable in your role so that you are relaxed and authentic, and invite your participants to relax and be as authentic and comfortable as possible. Also, I advise students to keep a notepad handy, not only to make notes during the interview, for probes and follow-up questions, but also to document what was said after the recorder was turned off. Often participants reveal the most important information after the interview is formally over. I advise students to write down everything they can remember after they turned off the recorder so that they can use the information for follow-up questions and deeper inquiry.

Selecting Your Conversational Style: Interactive Exercise

The following exercise is created for you to practice with a friend to identify your interview style. Find a friend who can speak with you for 15 minutes. Your task in these 15 minutes is to ask your friend how her/his weekend was. You have the freedom to approach this task any way that you feel comfortable. After conducting the task, complete the following worksheet.

How did you prepare for the interview if at all?

What kinds of questions did you ask, open-ended, closed-ended? Which did you ask more, open-ended or closed-ended questions? Did you let the participant ask you questions?

List some of your questions below. Do they elicit stories and experiences of the participant, or opinions?

What did you feel most comfortable about during the interview process?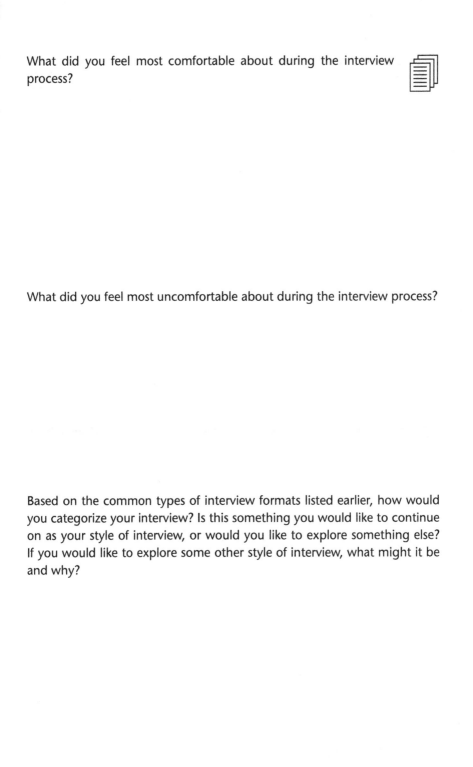

What did you feel most uncomfortable about during the interview process?

Based on the common types of interview formats listed earlier, how would you categorize your interview? Is this something you would like to continue on as your style of interview, or would you like to explore something else? If you would like to explore some other style of interview, what might it be and why?

What would you do differently next time if you were to conduct this interview?

What would you do similarly next time if you were to conduct this interview?

The Interview Process

While every interview can be unique and various theoretical perspectives might drive interviews differently, there are some common elements of an interview. For some this might be extremely basic information, while others might appreciate the documentation of the process as a demystification exercise.

1. After selecting participants and obtaining informed consent, if possible, meet the participant for a coffee or an informal chat about the study. Allow the conversation to be natural, where there is a flow in conversation with ample opportunities for the participant to ask you questions. Take the time to get a sense of the participant, how s/he responds to silence, how you respond to his/her silence, how you handle sharing information with each other, to help you build a rapport and inform subsequent interviews.

2. Schedule a date or set of dates for your interview(s). Make sure that you give yourself time in between interviews to conduct transcription and preliminary data analysis to inform yourself about meaningful questions to ask in subsequent interviews.

3. Prepare for the interview. Even if you are planning on conducting conversational interviews or elicitation interviews, write down for yourself what it is that you want to focus on specifically as you engage in an open-ended conversation. If you are conducting semistructured open-ended interviews, have about 4–5 open-ended questions for an hour of interview with some listing of follow-up probes that you could potentially use. (This is often the most common type of interview in which my students engage, as they feel comfortable having some questions in hand.)

4. Conduct the interview. At the end of the interview, thank the participant and inform the participant of the next steps in the process. This could be a follow-up meeting for transcription check, verification of preliminary analysis, and/or a second interview. However, as mentioned before, it is critical to transcribe and conduct preliminary analysis prior to subsequent interviews.

5. Transcribe the interview. While there are transcription services available, I will encourage you to conduct your own transcription to get close to the data. While transcribing, take notes on your thoughts, hunches, emotions, connections you are making to existing literature, theoretical perspectives, etc.

6. Conduct preliminary data analysis. If there is information collected from other data sources related to your research question, then compare your findings to the other sources of data collected. Are they similar? Are they different? Where might you need more information? Design questions for the second interview. Repeat Steps 1–6.

Types of Interview Questions

There are various ways of asking questions during the interviews. Your theoretical perspective, research purpose and questions, and information gained from literature review should guide your construction of interview questions. However, since qualitative research, to a large extent, is about reconstructing narratives shared by participants, the best interviews are those that help generate rich, thick descriptive stories, which contribute to an in-depth understanding of the topic of your study.

I have found tremendous value in Spradley's (1979) approach to interview questions for beginners in the field. Therefore, I am presenting Spradley's (1979) work from *The Ethnographic Interview* below as your guide to various types of interview questions. I want to encourage you to seek other options as you might benefit from them.

Descriptive Questions

These questions are designed to generate conversations about a specific incident with descriptive details. X = topic of your research.

- Tell me about a time when you experienced X.
- Tell me about the time when you first learned about X.
- Can you think of a time when you experienced X, and tell me about it in as much detail as you can remember?

Grand Tour Questions

These questions are designed for the participant to offer details about their everyday experiences in a particular setting.

- Can you describe a typical day in your life as X?
- Walk me through a typical day in your life as you experience X.

Specific Grand Tour Questions

These are similar to the grand tour questions listed above. Instead, these questions probe into a very specific incident and require the participant to offer descriptive details about the specific incident and how they experienced the specific incident.

- Can you describe what happened at class last night from the moment you arrived till you left?

Task-Related Grand Tour Questions

These are also similar to the tour questions listed above, but these tour questions are grounded in a specific task. An interviewer could ask the interviewee to draw, outline events, or do some other task that is relevant in the context of the study and then generate a conversation based on the task.

- Could you draw me a timeline of critical milestones in your life and tell me more about them?

Mini Tour Questions

These are like grand tour experience questions, but they deal with a more specific, smaller unit of experiences.

- Can you describe what you do when you take a break from your training sessions?

Example Questions

These questions are generated to discuss examples of an experience. Often participants might speak in general or abstract terms. As an interviewer, you would be benefited if you could understand the participant's experiences by hearing an example of the general, abstract, and analytical account.

- Can you give me an example of X?

Structural Questions

These questions are designed to understand the structure of the environment within which the participants are making meaning of their experiences. These questions are usually those questions that attempt to understand the social and cultural structures of an organization. In an interview, the interviewer would combine descriptive, tour, example, and structural questions together to develop a rich understanding of how the participants make meaning of their experiences.

- You mentioned that there are lots of secrets that are part of this organization. What are some of these secrets? (Then you go into a descriptive question to get stories.)
- Let us go back to what you were saying about the ways children are cared for in this daycare. You mentioned personal attention, conferences with parents, engaging activities, reporting when abuse is suspected. Can you think of other ways that you provide personal care and tell me about it?

- Can you tell me some typical phrases I would have heard if I was one of the first Black students in an all-White university?

Contrast Questions

Contrast questions are driven by the notions of falsification, a concept discussed in unit two. These questions are designed to disprove something that is appearing salient in the participant's experiences. These questions can also be designed to generate an alternate perspective so that the interviewer can challenge his or her perspective, subjectivities about the research topic. In other words, if you believe that the participant has continuously experienced discrimination in his or her experience, a contrast question would seek examples of times when the participant did not experience discrimination. This type of questioning allows for opening up a conversational space that explores an alternate perspective to add richness to understanding the participant's experiences.

- Earlier you mentioned that you experienced sadness, especially when it was associated with a negative situation. As we talked further, you said sometimes when you overcome negative situations and handle it well, you feel happy about how you choose to think about that situation. Can you talk about the times you felt happy about a negative situation after you overcame the challenges? (This is where you look at contradictory information and seek clarification.)
- You mentioned some of the difficulties you experienced during your training at this workplace. Can you think of some things during your training that worked well for you? (Falsification)

Examples of Interview Questions from Wiki Study

The following are some interview questions that were part of my wiki study. I have identified the types of questions to help crystallize your understanding.

1. Can you think of the first time when you used our wiki for the class project and tell me about it? (Descriptive question)
2. Tell me about a time when you specifically used the discussion thread on the wiki page for this class project in as much detail as you can remember. (Descriptive question)
3. Walk me through a typical session where you worked on your project using wiki in as much detail as you can remember. (Grand tour question)
4. Walk me through a session where you felt challenged using the wiki for the class project in as much detail as you can remember. (Specific grand tour question)
5. Please draw me a timeline of critical moments in learning as you participated in the wiki project. (Task-related grand tour question)
6. What might be some common phrases or concerns I would see if I looked over the discussion thread where you and your peers negotiated what to put as wiki content? (Structural question)
7. You mentioned that you felt challenged when this project did not have a specific structure for evaluation and you were asked to design your own evaluation rubric. Can you think of a time where designing your own evaluation rubric was helpful to your learning? (Alternate perspective)
8. Please give me an example of a learning experience that stands out to you as a result of participating in this wiki project. (Example question)

Design Your Interview: Interactive Exercise

Write some interview questions relevant to your study using Sprad-ley's categories described earlier. Identify the alignment of the question with other parts of your study (research purpose, questions, literature review, and/or theoretical framework).

TABLE 6.1

Interview Questions	Alignment

Tips and Strategies for Conducting Qualitative Interviews

Below are some rudimentary tips and strategies to help you get started in conducting qualitative interviews. As you discover your interview style, you might want to document tips and strategies for yourself in your research journal that work best for you. These tips are generated from my experience and those suggested by others (deMarrais, 2004; Kvale & Brinkmann, 2009; Spradley, 1979). See an example of a partially transcribed interview from my wiki project in Appendix A.

Keep your interview questions short and conversational in nature. Avoid long-winded interview questions that are so jargon-filled that by the time you complete the question, the interviewee is confused about the intent of the question.

Limit one point of inquiry per question. Use each interview question to explore one topic instead of combining multiple topics and lines of inquiry in one question. This will help in establishing clarity for yourself and the participant.

Ask more open-ended questions instead of closed-ended questions. Closed-ended questions are appropriate for verification purposes, but open-ended questions allow you to gain some perspective on how the participant constructs her understanding about her experiences. This allows you to gather rich details, which is difficult to do with closed-ended questions that have fixed answers.

Offer specific directions in your questions. If you want to know something specifically, then ask it directly, instead of making the question too broad. Sometimes questions are too broad, vague, abstract, general, and do not have the ability to generate specific details of an experience or event.

Be mindful of your subjectivities. While interviews are co-constructed narratives, be mindful of the role your subjectivities play as you design your interview questions and conduct your interviews.

Be present during the interview. It is important to be an active listener and to be present during the interview instead of thinking of the next question to ask. This will allow you to identify areas to probe further and develop a deep understanding.

Be comfortable with silence. Sometimes it is uncomfortable if the participant is silent after you have asked your question. Be at peace with the silence. Don't jump in and rephrase your questions, or try to answer the questions for the participant. Let the participant tell you what s/he needs.

Be mindful of nonverbal communication. It is important that your body language indicates you are interested in the participant's stories, that you're listening actively, and that you find value in what is being shared. Too much shifting in your seat, breaking eye contact, folded arms, looking around, leaning way back in your chair instead of forward could send the wrong message to the participant. Instead, lean forward a bit, do not break eye contact, jot down key words or phrases for probes to be used later, and demonstrate attention by not looking around and fidgeting in your seat.

Practice Makes Perfect: Interactive Exercise

For this exercise, you can select a person that could be aligned with your research interest, with whom you can conduct an authentic 15–20 minute interview. Alternatively, you can practice using the directions below if you do not have a participant lined up based on your research interest.

1. Select a person with whom you could speak about a key event that occurred during the past week that stayed with the person.
2. Prepare for a 15–20 minute interview.
3. Reflect on what theoretical perspective you might want to take while you approach this interview. What lens will you use to inform your understanding? What would be the key tenets?
4. Decide what style of interview you would like to engage in with the participant. Would you want the interview to be an elicited interview or a conversational one, or a semistructured open-ended one?
5. Write down broad framing questions or focal points for the interview.
6. Schedule and conduct the interview.
7. Transcribe the interview.
8. Respond to the prompts that follow this question.

What was different for you this time conducting a qualitative interview compared to the last time?

What worked well for you in this interview?

Where did you struggle in this interview?

How would you do this interview in the future? Would you keep everything the same? Try another technique? Write your questions differently? Watch more mindfully some aspects of behavior that you engaged in this time?

What Are Observations?

Observations are another form of data collection method in qualitative research. Generally speaking researchers engage in some kind of observer role within the context of the study. The documentation of information during observation is commonly known as field notes. The role of the observer varies based on the study and the researcher's positionality. The researcher can choose to be intimately involved in the setting that s/he observes or remain as an inactive member, akin to being a fly on the wall.

Dewalt and Dewalt (2002) identify three broad roles of participant observation that a researcher can play, which is a combination of earlier works of scholars. These roles are peripheral membership, active membership, and full membership.

Peripheral membership—the researcher is minimally involved in the group that s/he observes and does not participate in any activities but documents what s/he observes from the sidelines. The cultural insiders are familiar with this researcher and the reason for the researcher's presence.
Active membership—the researcher takes on some of the roles of the group that s/he observes and participates in some activities and observes others from the sidelines as a peripheral member. The cultural insiders are aware of the researcher's intent, presence, and role.
Full membership—the researcher is a fully active member of the group that s/he is observing. In many instances, the researcher participates as if s/he was a core member of the group that s/he is observing. The researcher participates in all activities, and the cultural insiders are aware of the researcher's intent, presence, and role.

The Observation Process

The following guidelines offer an overview of the process of conducting observations. Remember when conceptualizing your own process, consider your positionality and alignment with other parts of the study to be rigorous.

1. First you have to **gain access** to the community/culture/space that you would like to observe. Sometimes you might know one member from the community who can vouch for you and give you access. Other times you might have to volunteer contact, establish some rapport and trust, understand protocols, and gain confidence of a gatekeeper of the group before gaining access.
2. Part of establishing trust is being willing to answer questions asked of you, also known as **reciprocity**. This means that people might want to know the reason for your study, how you will use information, what kind of information you will collect, and how you will disseminate information. Sometimes researchers are asked personal information such as religious and political

beliefs, sexual orientations, etc. While it might feel strange to be at the other side of interrogation, know the cultural norms ahead of time so that you can be respectful when answering these questions. Never lie; always be honest and sincere.

3. Sometimes as part of reciprocity and your presence in the community, you might be asked to give back to the community. This could include purchase of material objects, offering transportation to members of the group, or something else. Again, it is important to know some of the cultural expectations ahead of time to determine your boundaries.

4. You will gain more insights the more you can adopt the group's shared norms and cultural behaviors. This will make you understand the perspectives of the members of the group in an intimate manner.

5. When in the field, take some note-taking device such as a digital tool like a computer, tablet, or a paper-based product such as a journal or a notepad.

6. Take as many notes as you can, and expand your fieldnotes immediately within the same night of the data collection so that you do not forget any important detail.

Tips and Strategies for Conducting Participant Observations

The following is a basic set of guidelines to conduct participant observations. For more information, refer to the resource list at the back of this book.

1. One of the first things to do while conducting participant observations is to map the space that you are observing. You do not have to be an artist, but try to get a sense of the space. Where are people gathered? How are people gathered? What objects are in the space? How are the objects situated? For example, in one of my projects, I observed a group of people playing trivia every week at a sports bar. The following is my initial mapping of the space and objects.

Next, I mapped the actors at the place where I sat and the space and objects surrounding our immediate environment.

2. Where possible, count how many people are gathered, around how many objects, so that it will allow you to paint a rich, accurate picture later on when you incorporate these details in your findings.

3. While writing down your notes, make sure you document your hunches, emotional reactions, and any subjectivities that you can identify.

4. Keep a time stamp on what you are observing and when in your field notes. This will allow you to understand a chronological progress of events.

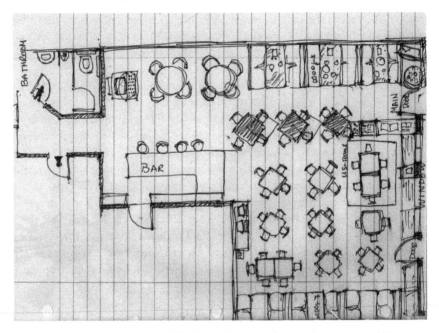

FIGURE 6.1 Initial Mapping of Sports Bar in a Participant Observation Project

FIGURE 6.2 Mapping of Actors in a Sports Bar Playing Trivia in a Participant Observation Project

5. When you first observe, you might find that you are making broad observations. However, as you continue your research, sharpen your focus of observation.

Of course if you are able to take a picture, then the mapping process is much easier, although you have to become attentive to various details.

Example of participant observation—Refer to Appendix B for a typical day vignette that resulted from my participant observation study of the trivia group as mentioned before.

Conducting Your Own Observations: Interactive Exercise

For this exercise, you will conduct an observation in a public space or a space that could be relevant to your research study. Public spaces could be a park, coffee shop, shopping mall, or a context that is more relevant to your research. You will play the role of a peripheral member in this setting. Be in the setting for at least 15–20 minutes. Carry with you some note-taking device and make sure that you expand your field notes immediately within return.

- Create a map of the space with objects and actors.
- Take a panoramic view of the space and describe it in as much detail as you can, engaging all your senses.
- If time permits, document some actions between actors.
- Document your thoughts, hunches, emotions, and impressions for now.
- You are welcome to use any format you like to keep your notes, but I offer a format below for your use. Divide your field notes into three specific sections: time, event/details, and impressions.

TABLE 6.2

Time	Event/Details	Impressions

After conducting the observations, answer the following questions (use your journal if you need additional space).

What information were you able to gather when you were observing?

What did you choose to focus on and why?

What did you ignore and why?

What level of detail did you document in your observation?

What was especially challenging for you conducting these observations?

What would you do similarly or differently going forward?

What Are Documents in Qualitative Research?

In qualitative research, documents are used regularly to offer contextual and deep understanding of the topic being studied. These documents could be things such as policies, lesson plans, participants' journals, letters, websites, or even visual materials such as photos. Documents can also include multimedia resources, such as audio and video data, in which case the researcher can call such pieces of information existing information. The driving force behind collecting documents is an awareness of your study, your positionality, and what might be some helpful information to collect that currently exists in the context of your study.

The Process of Collecting Documents

1. Before you start your study, make a list of all the documents you will need.
2. Beside each document listed, make a note of the reason why the document might be of interest to you.
3. Before starting the study, discuss with your potential participant about the list of documents that you are interested in and obtain consent.
4. Ask your participants if there are other potential relevant documents or existing data that could be helpful for your study, and seek consent for gathering those documents.

Example of Documents Collected in Wiki Study and Trivia Study

During my wiki studies, I collected students' assignments, information on the wiki pages, information on the discussion threads. These data sources allowed me to compare information the participants shared with me during interviews and my observation notes. Discrepancies became sites of further inquiry in the study.

In my trivia study, I collected existing data that were rules and policies for trivia, restaurant menu, trivia awards, and scoring rubric. These data sources allowed me an understanding of the trivia culture and the rules within which the participants were performing.

Tips and Strategies for Collecting Documents

1. Remain open about what could be potential sources of information for your study. Be creative about these sources.
2. Protect any identifying details in the document so that sensitive information about people remains confidential.
3. Connect information gathered from the documents or existing data to other data sources as well as reflect on how the information gathered from the documents or existing data informs your research questions and aligns with theoretical perspective and literature review.

Collecting Documents: Interactive Exercise

In the table below, list all the potential documents or data sources that might be of value to you for your research topic. Then align it with a reason why that source will be valuable. Reflect on how you are connecting the data source to theoretical perspective, research questions, or literature review. For example, if you want to collect lesson plans, perhaps you find value in it because information in lesson plans might provide information about instructional strategies and preparation efforts which is part of your research question. Perhaps there is literature that reveals specific information on instructional strategies and preparation and you want to compare the information gathered from your study with what is stated in the literature. Finally, perhaps your theoretical perspective leads you to believe that the curriculum and instruction is not as responsive to relating to students of color as they are to the dominant population. Perhaps a thorough analysis of documents could be a way to document how such privileging of dominant sensibilities are materialized in the classroom.

TABLE 6.3 Document Collection and Research Design

Document List	Reason for Selecting This Source	Connection to Other Parts of the Study (Research Questions, Theory, Literature Review)

Golden Nuggets: Interactive Exercise

As a summative activity, list your research questions on the left-hand side. List all potential data sources that can inform the research questions. Think about how the potential information in the data sources could connect to other parts of the study such as theoretical perspective and literature review. Perhaps some interview questions explore an area that needs further inquiry as stated by the literature. Perhaps some interview questions explore how participants experience inequity, connecting to some aspect of a critical theory framework. If you cannot think of the connections, do not worry. Come back to it later when your thinking on theoretical framework or literature review has crystallized.

TABLE 6.4

Research Questions	Data Source	Connection to Other Parts of the Study (Theory, Literature Review)

7

UNIT 7: DATA ANALYSIS, INTERPRETATION, AND RE-PRESENTATION

By now you have an understanding of qualitative research, how to frame your research purpose and questions, how to think with theory in your study, what subjectivities inform your study, what methodological design most appeals to you, and what methods of data collection might be appropriate for your study. You may have even collected some preliminary pilot data to explore your understanding of your research topic. It is time to make some sense of data collected and understand some approaches of data analysis in qualitative research.

Intentions of This Unit

In this unit, learners will explore two broad types of inductive data analysis processes used in qualitative research, although many more exist. The focus of the unit is to offer some guidelines and pathways to learners instead of offering prescriptive steps to data analysis.

What Does Data Analysis Mean?

There are different ways in which one can approach data management and analysis in qualitative research. However, whatever one's approach is, there should be adequate depth and justification to detail how one was able to identify findings in one's study. Data management and analysis occurs throughout one's study, and some would even say (depending on what is counted as data) that these processes could start even before the actual execution of research. Data management is the process through which the researcher manages a large volume of data. Often this process could include chunking small analytic units from the larger body of raw data for closer analysis. Data analysis involves creating processes that would allow for deep insights that reflect how the researcher integrated theoretical and analytical frameworks, previous understanding of literature, and the focus of the research purpose and questions. These deep insights can often lead to identification of findings in a qualitative study.

What Is Inductive Analysis?

Inductive analysis in qualitative research refers to working "up" from the data. The process of inductive analysis assumes that the researcher is not starting the data analysis with any kind of preestablished testable hypothesis about the data. Inductive analysis is the process through which a qualitative researcher might look at all the raw data, chunk them into small analytical units of meaning for further analysis (usually called codes), cluster similar analytical units and label them as categories, and identify salient patterns after looking within and across categories (usually called themes). While conducting data analysis, the researcher often maintains a journal to reflect on subjectivities, emotions, hunches, questions that arise, and ways in which s/he is making sense of the data in association with theoretical, methodological, analytical framework, and research purpose and questions.

An Approach to Inductive Analysis

There are many ways in which inductive analysis can be conducted and several volumes of texts are written about these ways. In this section, I present a synthesis that represents a conglomeration of suggestions offered, intersected with my sensibilities and preferences.

Inductive analysis or any other form of data analysis is iterative. What that means is that there is no defined linear format through which analysis occurs. The researcher moves back and forth between various stages and processes. Broadly speaking inductive analysis should include the following guidelines:

- Familiarize yourself with data (read and re-read your data several times).
- Use writing as a form of inquiry for various questions that arise, for understanding data, for analyzing smaller chunks of data, for connecting various data pieces, etc.
- Chunk data into manageable units of analysis (coding). You can do this by pulling out phrases, sentences, paragraphs that stand out to you. You then have the option of labeling what you have pulled out as your standout pieces. These labels could be descriptive, theoretical, emotional, reflective of your subjectivities, etc. Or you can just leave the pieces that stand out to you as is, without labeling to write around those pieces.
- Write about your chunking process, theoretical, topical, and/or methodological ideas that are taking shape, things that are morphing for you in the

study, further questions that are arising for you as a result of reflecting on your chunking process.

- Cluster some of the analytical units into categories (broader groups with a descriptive label) based on whatever you consider is appropriate. Sometimes this clustering is based on meaning, critical incidents, theoretical constructs, or patterns from existing literature review.
- Write about your clustering process, theoretical, topical, and/or methodological ideas that are taking shape, things that are morphing for you in the study, further questions that are arising for you as a result of reflecting on your chunking process.
- Look across and within categories to identify patterns that arise to the surface for you. Ask methodological, topical, and theoretical questions of these patterns to analyze these patterns in depth.
- Write reflexively about pattern identification and the connection you are making to other parts of your research (research purpose, questions, theoretical framework, methodology, research in your field). Look for silences, contradictions, and tensions.
- Discuss your process and findings with a peer.
- Discuss your findings with your participants.
- Modify and revisit any of the abovementioned suggestions as many times as necessary.

Do Themes Really Emerge?

Often you will hear people use the term "emergent themes" implying that the themes "emerge" from the data. Do themes actually emerge out of the data on their own? Of course not! You identify themes out of your own analytical thinking. As you work closely with your data, you begin to see patterns, which inform the way you identify themes. These patterns are organizational, characterize different segments of data, and help the researcher and the reader develop an in-depth understanding that responds to the research questions and purpose.

An Example of Inductive Analysis

Recall my wiki study. In that study, I incorporated an inductive analytical approach. In the published article (http://thenjournal.org/index.php/then/article/view/48/47), I described my process of data analysis, which mirrored the iterative process of inductive analysis shared earlier. I became extremely familiar with the data, chunked the data into analytical units, wrote around my chunking of the data, wondered about what I was trying to understand and what insights I was gaining to ultimately identify three salient patterns. Below I present an abbreviated outline of one of my themes, categories, and codes. Please note that even though this outline is presented in linear form, the process and understanding was much messier than it is presented here. The outline reflects what claims I was comfortable making and what I was using to support my claim. The first-level heading reflects a theme, the second-level heading reflects a category, and the third-level heading reflects a code (often a direct excerpt from the transcript or a descriptive label I assigned).

Anxiety about academic performance is not about performance.

1. Academic grades

    a. Earning a grade versus getting a grade
    b. Anxious anyway, no matter what was said
    c. Prior academic experiences

2. Pleasing the teacher

    a. Is this what you want?
    b. We have to create our own rubric
    c. Don't want to let you down

3. High expectations of self

    a. I always do well in anything I try
    b. Feedback sometimes makes me question myself
    c. Wanted to get most out of graduate school

4. New way of learning

    a. Prior learning experiences
    b. Floundering in darkness without structured learning
    c. Active learning is empowering, eventually

As you can see from the above outline, even if you did not know much about my study, you can have a general idea of what might be some ideas that stood out to me from working with the students, listening to their interviews, and from other data sources, in alignment with other parts of the research. You could probably sense that the students experienced anxiety and it was not just because of the grade. You could probably see that students' experiences of anxiety included their experience from previous academic training, ways they learned before, needing to please the teacher, and having high expectations of self. When they had to negotiate all these tensions while learning new content, in a different way, holding themselves to high standards, they had anxiety that was not only about performance but also about something much more than performance. A good thematic outline should have depth and offer some indication about how the researcher is making connections between codes, categories, and themes.

Analyzing by Doing: Interactive Exercise

By now you should have some transcript from the interview you conducted as part of an activity in the previous unit. Depending on what observation activity you engaged in, you might even have relevant observation data related to your research topic. Use the guidelines presented earlier for an approach to inductive analysis to work through your data sources to at least conduct a preliminary analysis of data and identify at least one theme, associated categories and codes. I have listed the guideline below once more for you to follow.

- Familiarize yourself with data (read and re-read your data several times).
- Use writing as a form of inquiry for various questions that arise, for understanding data, for analyzing smaller chunks of data, for connecting various data pieces, etc.
- Chunk data into manageable units of analysis (coding). You can do this by pulling out phrases, sentences, paragraphs that stand out to you. You then have the option of labeling what you have pulled out as your stand-out pieces. These labels could be descriptive, theoretical, emotional, reflective of your subjectivities, etc. Or you can just leave the pieces that stand out to you as is, without labeling to write around those pieces.
- Write about your chunking process, theoretical, topical, and/or methodological ideas that are taking shape, things that are morphing for you in the study, further questions that are arising for you as a result of reflecting on your chunking process.
- Cluster some of the analytical units into categories (broader groups with a descriptive label) based on whatever you consider is appropriate. Sometimes this clustering is based on meaning, critical incidents, theoretical constructs, or patterns from existing literature review.
- Write about your clustering process, theoretical, topical, and/or methodological ideas that are taking shape, things that are morphing for you in the study, further questions that are arising for you as a result of reflecting on your chunking process.
- Look across and within categories to identify patterns that arise to the surface for you. Ask methodological, topical, and theoretical questions of these patterns to analyze these patterns in depth.
- Write reflexively about pattern identification and the connection you are making to other parts of your research (research purpose, questions, theoretical framework, methodology, research in your field). Look for silences, contradictions, and tensions.

- Discuss your process and findings with a peer.
- Discuss your findings with your participants.
- Modify and revisit any of the abovementioned suggestions as many times as necessary.

List your thematic outline with at least one theme, categories, and codes below:

What worked well for you and what were your challenges?

Mapping as Inductive Analysis

Sometimes the coding, categorizing, and thematizing approach might not suit one's ways of thinking and processing information. This is especially critical to be aware of because the more you can align your ways of processing information to your analytic approach, the higher your chances of developing in-depth insights. Figure 7.1 is a combination of mapping and writing as inquiry that could help with data analysis.

The process in Figure 7.1 is iterative, meaning the researcher moves in and out of several steps. The key to this kind of process is writing around various chunks of data and making connections. For example, I would read interview transcripts, and when there would be a turn in the story the participant was telling me, I would stop and then start to write around that chunk of the transcript. I would reflect on thoughts that were rising to the surface for me, based on what I was reading. I would ask myself the following questions:

- What is going on here?
- What connections am I making?
- How does my theoretical framing make me think of this excerpt?
- How does what I am reading connect to the literature in the field?
- How does what I am reading connect to the research purpose?
- What truths/realities/meanings are rising to the surface for me?
- What contradictions/tensions/messiness are rising to the surface for me?
- Where do I need to probe further?
- What hunches are arising for me?

I would then re-read the data sources and repeat the process. After several rounds of this process, I would start writing about the connections I was making between several chunks of data and my reflections about those chunks. Most of the time this was a nonlinear process of thinking. Because I am a visual learner, I would start mapping these connections visually. Then I would write and reflect about the map that I created. This process of writing as inquiry into my thoughts and connecting various parts of the data became extremely helpful when I had to write up findings (described in a later section). Figure 7.1 is an example of one of the concept maps I created while I was managing and analyzing my data. Recall in my study, I was working with two participants, Neerada and Yamini, who were from India, during their first year of graduate studies in the U.S.

You will see that for each branch, I had a theoretical construct with which I informed how I was thinking about the data and the participants' negotiations. So when you see words like transnationalism or colonial subject, think of them as my way of reminding myself that I have written around those ideas extensively in my journal when I was chunking the data and reflecting on those ideas as they related to the data. So, when I looked to connect between various parts of the data with my analytical insights, theoretical constructs, and literature in the field, I had

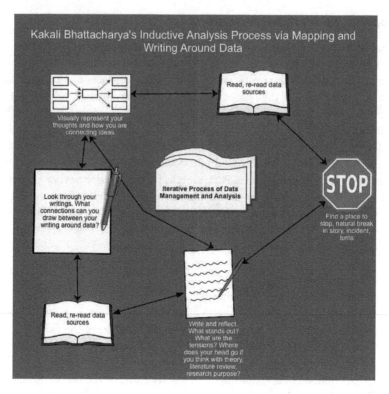

FIGURE 7.1 Inductive Analysis Via Mapping and Writing as Inquiry

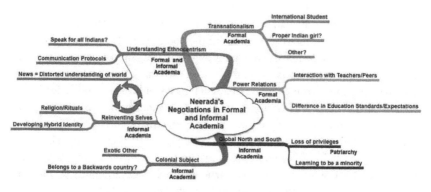

FIGURE 7.2 Mapping Neerada's Negotiations in Formal and Informal Academia

words as reminders about how I made the connections in addition to my writing around those connections. For example, when I labeled a branch in the figure as Global North and South, I was reminding myself of the literature review I had conducted on postcolonialism and transnationalism that was helping me to map the participants' experiences within a broader landscape.

Mapping, Writing, and Analyzing: Interactive Exercise

Use whatever data sources you have gathered by now (transcript, observations, artifacts) that are relevant to your topic. Follow the process outlined in Figure 7.1 and work through your data in chunks, writing, reflecting, connecting ideas, and mapping your understanding visually. Feel free to be as complex or simple as you want to be. Remember, this is work in progress so you can also add, change details.

Interpretation and Data Re-Presentation in Qualitative Research

Interpretation of qualitative research involves developing narratives about the ways in which the researcher is co-constructing meaning with her participants. Often this involves analyzing data, looking within various chunks of data, identifying analytical insights, and reflecting on the insights gained through some narrative format. These narrative formats are often rich, thick with contextual details, and help illuminate ideas about the topic the researcher is investigating. Then when the researcher represents these insights, an alignment with various parts of the study (epistemology, ontology, theoretical framework, methodology, literature review, etc.) becomes necessary to maintain rigor in a study.

There are many types of re-presentations in qualitative research. I say re-presentations because the participants' stories are re-presentations of what they told you during the interviews. You are not really able to represent anyone in his/her truest form. The best you can do is re-present the information shared with you while collaborating with the participant to co-construct the findings of the study. Some forms of re-presentations include:

i.   Thematic descriptions
ii.   Poetic representations
iii. Plays
iv.   Performances
v.   Documentaries
vi.   Musicals
vii. Novels
viii. Short stories
ix.   Photo essays
x.   Digital stories
xi.   A combination of any of the above.

The goal of these re-presentations is that they can be presented in either traditional or nontraditional format so that the material will be accessible. The best way to develop re-presentation skills is to read as many exemplars as possible and note in your journal what you like about those exemplars. Then start developing a writing practice where you're creating narratives reflecting your insights in your study. This way, when you're ready to put things together for presentation or publication, you would already have had reflected deeply on your ideas and how you have connected them to various parts of the study. In the next section I present to you an abbreviated format of connections between various parts of a study.

So how might you thread through the research hourglass to come to a re-presentation?

The following are examples of how to think about certain types of qualitative studies while maintaining alignment with epistemology, theoretical framework, methodology, and re-presentation.

Epistemology	Constructionism
Theoretical framework	Interpretivism
Methodology	Narrative analysis
Methods	Interviews, observations, documents, etc.
Re-presentation	Stories with excerpts from interviews, descriptive scenes developed from the observations, and integration of information from documents where relevant.
Epistemology	Constructionism
Theoretical framework	Symbolic interactionism
Methodology	Case study
Methods	Conversations, observations, photo elicitations
Re-presentation	Thematic narratives integrating excerpts from interviews, details from observations, with photos weaved into the narratives.
Epistemology	Constructionism
Theoretical framework	Phenomenology
Methodology	Phenomenology
Methods	Interviews, observations, documents, pictures
Re-presentation	Thematic description of the phenomenon being studied integrating information from data collected.
Epistemology	Constructionism
Theoretical framework	Feminism
Methodology	Autoethnography
Methods	Conversations, observations, elicitations
Re-presentation	Personal narrative within the context of the culture that is being studied. Rich, thick details combined about the author's experiences, introspective reflections about those experiences, and the mapping of those experiences within some broader cultural landscape.
Epistemology	Constructionism
Theoretical framework	Interpretivism
Methodology	Ethnography
Methods	Interviews, observations, documents, pictures
Re-presentation	A nonfiction with five chapters

The previous (limited) breakdown of the aligned re-presentations should give you an indication of the variety of approaches that one can take when making decisions about qualitative research. The rigor of the decision lies in being able to align the choices within the larger structure of the research design. Therefore, no matter what approach you choose for your research, remain open to any form of re-presentation.

Cautions about Choosing Re-Presentations

We have talked about the importance of lining up the choice of re-presentation within the research design. However, there are some cautionary notes that you need to pay attention to when selecting a genre of re-presentation.

1. Do not choose a genre of re-presentation without **studying the genre**. In other words, if you feel that narrative writing would be an appropriate choice for you, then study the genre of narrative writing instead of assuming that you can write narratives.
2. **Keep your choice simple.** Do not try to put in everything that you can think of just so that you have multiple forms of re-presentation. How can you say what you want to say in the most effective manner?
3. You need to **practice writing intensely** regardless of what genre you might want to choose for your re-presentation. For the purpose of dissertation, or a residency project, or a research paper, or a conference presentation, no matter what your genre is, you are responsible to make an argument for it, describe your genre, and make your writing come alive. Your words should dance on paper, create beautiful pictures, and evoke people simultaneously. This takes practice, and you should start early on and make many drafts.
4. **Do not be afraid to play** with multiple types of re-presentations. Just because you choose one form doesn't mean you have to stick to it forever or even for that particular research. Try other types of analysis and re-presentations and see which fits the best. I remember trying at least four different kinds of re-presentations before I finally settled on one for my dissertation.

Re-Presenting Your Study

There are a few considerations you need to keep in mind when you write up your study. Since writing will be a key part of your study, it is important to pay attention to how you want to utilize writing to re-present your study.

1. **SHOW, NOT TELL.** You need to let the data do the talking instead of you "telling" people how to think about the data. Present the data in its complexities and contradictions. Let the reader figure out what they want to figure out instead of you "telling" them what to figure out. Expect that the reader is an active participant of this re-presentation.
2. Know who your **audience**(s) might be. Do not limit yourself to one type of audience, i.e. academia. Your research should have value beyond academia. Therefore, consider how you would present research to people who are outside of academia who will also be benefited by your study.

3. Know how you are **converting your data into evidence**. What decisions did you make to decide the ways in which some portions of the data were evidence and others were not?
4. Select a set of key events, critical incidents, epiphanic moments, turning points in your findings as ways to represent. These **critical moments** can themselves become the sites of analysis in their tensions, contradictions, and ambiguities.
5. Present your **own negotiations**, decisions that you had to make, turning points, and participation in the research. Excerpts from your researcher journal highlighting reflective thoughts, hunches, and preliminary identification of meanings should also be part of the presentation. Therefore, the reader can follow along with your interpretation and negotiations in order to understand why and how you came to your conclusions.
6. Use as many **visual forms of re-presentations** of your data analysis and findings as would be appropriate and necessary. Even though qualitative researchers like stories and narratives, visual display of data in the form of tables, diagrams, maps, and models offer tremendous clarity to the reader. Also, by trying to identify appropriate forms of visual display of the data, your research becomes sharper and so too does your thinking around your research.

But Writing Is Hard

Sometimes it is extremely difficult to know what you want to write and how to write. You might be scared that your writing might not be academic enough, or that you might not represent the participants' stories accurately, or that you are too overwhelmed with your findings and do not know where to start. Below are some tips that might be of use to you:

*   Conduct some free writing exercises. Free writing exercises are where you start to write, for your eyes only, and do not correct spelling or grammar, but continue to write your thoughts down as it comes to you without judgment. Then you can go back and read over what you wrote to identify salient points. You could also use prompts like:

    i.   What is the key issue here?
    ii. What do I know for sure?
    iii. One thing that I definitely have evidence for is . . .
    iv. This study is really about . . .
    v.   What I don't understand is . . .
    vi. What is going on with my study is . . .

*   Treat each paragraph as a mini essay with thesis sentence, body, and a concluding sentence addressing the thesis sentence and transitioning to the

paragraph following. This will allow you to maintain a flow in your writing. When you're done, print your work, and beside each paragraph jot down the key argument you are trying to make. Then decide if these arguments have logical consistency and flow.

- Look through your writing to avoid repetitions. If you have explained and elaborated an idea once, then you do not need to do it in another way later. Sometimes the writing is done in phases and we forget what we wrote before. This is why editing is critical in your work. Make sure you have someone else other than yourself look over your work for editing purposes.

- Vary sentence structure and length. Avoid run-on complicated sentences as much as possible. Watch out for words used excessively. Avoid writing in passive voice as much as possible. Pay attention to your word choices and use strong verbs where necessary.

- If you use metaphors, make sure that you have developed metaphors appropriately so that it does not appear that the use of the metaphor was superficial.

- Make sure whatever you produce as your findings and discussion of your findings are aligned with your research purpose and questions. This will add clarity and sharpen your focus of your study.

- Save copies of your previous drafts as you might have ideas in there that you could use later or might want to revisit for elaboration. Sometimes it is easy to think that only the current revised version is the only one with merit. However, you might have information in earlier drafts, such as a quote, a citation, etc., that could be useful later.

- Wait till you finish your entire paper, thesis, or dissertation to write your abstract. This will help you with clarity and focus.

- Make sure that you do not finalize a title until after you have completed your work. It is acceptable to have a working title in place as you work on the content of your work.

- Be mindful of the concluding statements you make so they do not overly assert things for which you did not have evidence in your study. It is better to remain conservative in your conclusion and leave room for multiple possibilities to be explored further. Focus on what you attempted to do, what you were able to discover, and what questions your findings point to for other research projects. You can also offer recommendations, implications for key stakeholders, and personal reactions if you feel it's necessary to do so.

Identifying Sample Re-Presentation Exemplars: Interactive Exercise

Given that people would have varied research interests, it is difficult to offer what might be an exemplar for you. You are welcome to select your own article as an exemplar or select one from the following list to read as an exemplar and then respond to the prompts.

Chaudhry, L. (2000). Researching "my people," researching myself; fragments of a reflexive tale. In E.A. St. Pierre & W.S. Pillow (Eds.), *Working the ruins: Feminist poststructural research and practice in education* (pp. 96–113). New York, NY: Routledge.

Geertz, C. (1973). Deep play: Notes on the Balinese Cockfight. *Daedalus*, Winter, 1–38.

Purser, G. (2009). The dignity of job-seeking men: Boundary work among immigrant day laborers. *Journal of Contemporary Ethnography*, *38*(1), 117–139.

Rhoads, R.A. (1995). Whale tales, dog piles, and beer goggles: An ethnographic case study of fraternity life. *Anthropology and Education Quarterly*, *26*(3): 306–323.

While you read the article, make notes on the following:

- Paper structure and sections within the paper

- Paragraph structure and connection between paragraphs

- Researcher voice

- Choice of representation genre

- Research purpose and questions

- Theoretical and methodological framework

- Methodology

- Integration of data sources (What did you think were the data sources for the study?)

- Analytical insights

- Ways in which the author argued/justified/explained the choices made in the work

- Word choices that stand out

- Descriptive details about the context of the study

- Any metaphor use?

- Contradictions/tensions/meanings in multiplicities?

Based on your analysis of this exemplar, what are some things that you would like to incorporate in your re-presentation and why?

Golden Nuggets: Interactive Exercise

You are now prepared to conceptualize and execute your qualitative study. I leave you with this activity that might keep you inspired in your future academic journey. This activity was conducted by Kathleen deMarrais during my years in graduate school at the University of Georgia. I have adapted the activity to my teaching contexts.

Instructor Note: If you conduct this exercise with your students, then bring some rocks to class (I use polished rocks, but any would do), and give them a chance to select a rock that they like intuitively, without much analysis or time. Then conduct the research rock exercise, where the students have the rock in their hands and you read out the script.

Student Note: If you want to do this exercise outside of class on your own, then select your own rock and read through the script on your own, quietly, in a place where you will not be disturbed midway. Of course, you wouldn't be closing your eyes.

YOUR RESEARCH ROCK

Close your eyes. Take your rock in your hand and make a closed fist. Breathe in. Breathe out. Feel the rock in your hand. Is it smooth? Textured? A bit of both? Think of the color. The shape. From this day onward, this is your research rock.

I give you this gift of this research rock to carry with you as you continue on your research journey. This is a magical rock with special powers. To access this rock's special powers, have the rock close to you for the rest of your academic journey.

1. Hold your rock tightly in your hand as you think about your research topic. Think about why you care about this topic. Is it because of your personal experiences only? Have you done some literature review on your topic? Are you passionate about this topic? Can you stay interested in this topic for a significant amount of time?
2. Feel the rock in your hand as you consider your research purpose and questions. What is it that you really want to know? Do these questions really point to what you want to know? Are you able to engage meaningfully in this study? Is it feasible and realistic? Remember you do not have to solve the world's problems in one dissertation.

3. Move your finger over the rock as you think about the values, beliefs, assumptions you bring to the table. What is your personal investment in this topic? Why are you professionally invested in this topic? This is your subjectivity rock.

4. Hold the rock tightly in your hand and think of it as your theoretical lens. Why did you choose this framework? What promises does this framework have? Where are you struggling with your understanding of theory? What do you understand well about your theory? Does your framework relate to the research purpose and questions? To the literature? To the methodology of your study?

5. Put your rock on top of your computer as you collect your data and transcribe, expand those field notes, and jot down your thoughts in your researcher journal. Let the rock remind you to write honestly and descriptively. Are you transcribing as soon as possible after the interview? Are you expanding the field notes as soon as possible after you conducted the observations? Are you keeping a researcher journal?

6. Hold your rock in your hands as you consider all your data sources. Think of ways you can develop insights across and within various data sources. What are some things that are common in all of the data sources? Where are the contradictions/tensions? What have you considered? What else do you need to consider? Where are you stuck?

7. As you conduct your interviews, hold your rock to help you focus, be present, and to listen actively. Remember to be thoughtful in your probes. Remember to be comfortable with silence. As you transcribe those interviews, do not throw your research rock at your computer. You will need them both. Be patient.

8. Hold your rock close to you every time you look at the pile of your raw data and feel overwhelmed about data analysis. Manage your data into small analytical pieces. Then look at each piece. Then connect your analysis together, chunk by chunk, pattern by pattern, to create your understanding. Do not rush or slap on a quick theme just because you see it as your first pattern. Be patient; trust the process.

9. Your rock is a writing rock because it can help you tell the story of your study. Think about what you know about your study. What are you trying to share? Remember to show, not tell. Use rich details to describe the participant, the site, events, and interactions. Use engaging strategies in your writing. Vary sentence structures. Use powerful, evocative words. We do not write the whole dissertation at once. We write a sentence. We write a paragraph. We write a section. We write a chapter. We write a dissertation. We finish.

10. Your rock is also your confidence rock when you present your research for your peers, professors, or your academic community. Keep the rock with you in your pocket. When you feel anxious or nervous, just touch the rock, and take a deep breath. Stay calm. Know that this is your study and you know the most about this study. Know that with your best work, you have nothing to worry about.

11. Open your eyes. Pay attention to how you feel in this moment. If you want to share your thoughts out loud, do so. If you want to journal about them, do so. Namaste.

8

UNIT 8: PULLING IT ALL TOGETHER

In the past units, you have been introduced to qualitative methods, theoretical frameworks, methodological approaches, methods of data collection, preliminary approaches to data analysis, and representation. We have worked through exercises in each unit to help you create and execute a small qualitative research project. In this unit, we will pull together everything you have learned as a summative activity for this book. You can also use this unit as a blueprint to design new qualitative studies and as a refresher.

Intentions of This Unit

In this unit, learners will be introduced to the ways of thinking that inform qualitative research design. This will be a unit that the students can revisit and reconceptualize their projects as they continue to crystallize their understanding about their research interests. Learners will interact with exercises that will allow them to expand their thinking on their research interest to engage closely with various aspects of research design.

Revisiting Your Research Interest

In this section, I invite you to revisit your topic as many times as you like, at various stages of your research design, data collection, analysis, and representation, to gain clarity or refocus when you get lost in the process of research. For my students, this has been a helpful revisiting spot when they are trying to collect data, design interview questions, identify various sources of data collection, deciding what to focus on when conducting observations, and when they got lost in data analysis.

Revisiting Your Research Interest: Interactive Exercise Continued. . .

What is it that you really want to know? What matters to you the most, makes your heart sing? (Avoid jargons as much as possible.)

Whose stories would you hear? What kind of stories would you hear?

How many people will you talk to? (Remember more does not mean better. Be realistic in thinking this number. More does not mean better. It could mean superficial.)

What will be the location of this study? (This can be where you collect all your data, where you analyze and write up your data.)

The purpose of this study is to . . .

The research questions guiding this study are (Make sure that your research questions are aligned with your research purpose above):

What terms/jargons do you need to operationalize/conceptualize? (List all the terms that could be broken down into simpler terms, with specific indicators.)

What theoretical perspective best fits your study and why?

Expand Your Thoughts about Your Research Project

In this section, we will dig deeper into your thoughts surrounding the research design that is appropriate for your research purpose and questions that you listed above. Remember, there is no right or wrong answer, but an honest engagement with your thoughts.

Research Design and Theoretical Alignment

In this section, we will explore your design in an even deeper manner and connect your design to the tenets of your theoretical perspective(s). Complete the following table to the best of your ability. If you are unable to answer some of the prompts, do not be hard on yourself. Just revisit this section when you are able to respond to the prompts. The process of qualitative research is iterative, so linear progression is not always necessary.

The first column lists certain motivations for conducting qualitative studies. If they align with yours, then think of the tenets of your theoretical perspective that align with such a motivation. The third column lists some methodologies that might be appropriate. This is an invitation for you to explore those methodologies further. If the methodologies listed in the third column do not match your thoughts or reasoning, then list your own methodology. It is important that your research reflects your thinking more than anyone else's prescribed pathways. The pathway is offered to you as an organizing strategy.

TABLE 8.1 Aligning Motivation, Theory, and Methodology

Motivation	Tenets of theoretical perspective(s)	Suggested methodology (Insert your own if you find a better match)
You're interested in understanding, describing, identifying an essence of a lived experience, a phenomenon.		Phenomenology
You're interested in exploring people's lived realities as they interact with other people in a group, setting, organization, etc.		In-depth interview study
Your interest lies in gaining a diverse set of perspectives from a small group of people with opportunities to probe and ask follow-up questions.		Focus-group study

(Continued)

TABLE 8.1 (Continued)

Motivation	Tenets of theoretical perspective(s)	Suggested methodology (Insert your own if you find a better match)
You're mostly interested in stories. You like hearing stories, you want to repeat your findings in some story structure and you want to hear stories about people's experiences surrounding an event, or their daily lives, or their interactions with people, event, organization, circumstances, etc.		Narrative inquiry
You're mostly interested in understanding the culture of a group of people, organization, setting, etc.		Ethnography (duration in field for at least 18 months) Critical ethnography (duration in field for at least 18 months) Visual ethnography (duration in field for at least 18 months)
You're interested in how communication occurs in various settings and how such communication leads to people's meaning making and experiences		Discourse analysis Ethnomethodology Conversation analysis
You want to talk to as many people as possible and snowball your sampling to as diverse a section of people who can contribute to your topic. You want to generate a theory out of your study.	NONE NEEDED HERE	Constructivist Grounded Theory
You want to draw a boundary around one central point of focus on your study, such as a person, organization, classroom, or project and gain as in-depth understanding as possible.		Case study
You love to analyze documents, archived materials, historical artifacts, from a particular time period that you wish were studied with further analysis and detail on a topic that interests you.		Historical research (mostly analysis of documents, material culture)

Motivation	Tenets of theoretical perspective(s)	Suggested methodology (Insert your own if you find a better match)
You value people's experiences about historical moments in the past and are concerned that certain kinds of experiences, if not documented will not provide the knowledge that is currently missing in our social documentary. You enjoy talking to people about their life histories, memories of critical past events, etc.		Oral history Life story Biography
You want to focus on your experiences within the context of a cultural narrative or a set of cultural narratives because you think that it is important to document your experiences in this way as it provides knowledge in a way that currently does not exist.		Autoethnography Life story
Add your own here		

Please note that the above list is not exhaustive and there are about as many combinations of intentions, theoretical tenets, and methodological alignments as you can imagine. Do not feel restricted by the choices above. You can feel free to align your intentions with your theoretical perspective and methodological choices as you see fit. Just make sure that you have some solid academic arguments for doing what you are doing.

Methods of Data Collection

Next is a table with some possible data collection sources and a space to document your interest and what kind of information you intend to gather from those potential data sources.

TABLE 8.2 Exploring Data Collection Methods

Potential Data Source	*Mark X if you want to use this source*	*What information/stories do you wish to obtain from this data source?*
Open-ended semistructured interviews (questions prepared and have room for probes based on participant's response).		
Open-ended initial question (Tell me about X the first time you experienced it in as much detail as you can), with follow-up questions based on participant's response.		
Conversational interviews, open-ended, informed by broad lines of inquiry, bidirectional, researcher shares information too about the topic.		
Focus group interviews (open-ended, semistructured, structured).		
Photo-elicited interviews (conversations generated from pictures taken/selected by the participant or the researcher).		
Object-elicited interviews (conversations generated from objects selected by the participant or the researcher).		
Other elicited interviews (maybe you would like your participant to complete a task, like draw a timeline of critical events and discuss experiences on the timeline).		
Participant observation (think about the role you will play while observing—active, passive, peripheral?).		
Documents (think about all the documents that would be relevant to understanding the context of your study better, such as policy manuals, lesson plans, daily planner, etc.).		
Websites (think about all the websites maybe the participant uses, or websites that are relevant to the context of the study with which the participant is familiar, etc.).		
Multimedia data (think of video clips, song lyrics, songs, etc., that might be relevant for your study).		

Potential Data Source	Mark X if you want to use this source	What information/stories do you wish to obtain from this data source?
Other data sources that might be relevant for your study that are not mentioned in the choices above.		

Data Analysis Methods

As with the previous sections, the options for data analysis presented below are abbreviated. However, your choice is strengthened when you can demonstrate an alignment between your epistemology, theoretical perspective(s), research purpose and questions, research design, data analysis, and data representation. I invite you to engage with the next activity to assess to what you might be naturally drawn. Then, revisit this section repeatedly as you immerse yourself deeper in your study to see if you need to recalibrate your preferences.

The first column will have room for you to enter your thoughts as you explore the activity presented next.

TABLE 8.3 Aligning Personal Preferences with Data Analysis

What I am naturally drawn to is . . .	You most probably will benefit from	Is there another approach that appeals to you? List below.
A systematic analysis, a path laid out in front of you, examples from other people, some linear progression of ideas, even though at times it might not be linear or clear.	Inductive analysis—systematically coding, sorting, categorizing, building some organizational structure, visualizing your data, constructing themes.	
Your thoughts?	Methodological approaches you could include but are not limited to: • Ethnography • Grounded theory • Case study • Interview study • Narrative inquiry • Critical ethnography	

(Continued)

TABLE 8.3 (Continued)

What I am naturally drawn to is . . .	You most probably will benefit from	Is there another approach that appeals to you? List below.
A systematic organization of all sorts of archived materials, documents, pictures, websites, etc., and looking for patterns within those materials. **Your thoughts?**	Content analysis—systematic organization of information, ideas presented in some form of commonly occurring pattern. You can use inductive approaches for analyzing data in this context too. Methodological approaches you could include but are not limited to: • Life history • Oral history • Historical study • Biographical study	
Telling stories, hearing stories, writing stories, looking for elements that make up a story. **Your thoughts?**	Narrative analysis—exploring your data with the intent to identify structures of a story. What structure you lean on depends on what theory of storytelling you are using in your study, as there are many ways to tell a story. Methodological approaches you could include but are not limited to: • Case study • Interview study • Oral history • Life history	

What I am naturally drawn to is . . .	You most probably will benefit from	Is there another approach that appeals to you? List below.
Thinking strongly with theory. Using theoretical tenets to read through the data and understand and make connections between different parts of the data that are tangibly collected and perhaps intangibly processed. **Your thoughts?**	Theory-driven analysis without any predetermined format but following a process of chunking material, writing around the material with theoretical reflections, and connecting between various chunks to obtain deeper understanding. Note that all analysis should ideally be incorporated with theoretical tenets, but the scholars who lean on this approach often reject the more traditional inductive approaches of codes, categories, and theme identification in preference of theory being the one and only guide for analysis. Methodological approaches you could include but are not limited to: • Case study • Interview study • Oral history • Life history • Narrative inquiry	
Finding a core essence. Analyzing all shared experience to find an invariant theme, a core essence of a particular phenomenological experience. **Your thoughts?**	Phenomenological analysis where certain data management processes are invoked for the purpose of phenomenological reduction in order to determine the structures and essence of a phenomenological experience. Methodological approaches you could include but are not limited to: • Case study • Interview study • Oral history • Life history • Narrative inquiry	

TABLE 8.3 (Continued)

What I am naturally drawn to is . . .	You most probably will benefit from	Is there another approach that appeals to you? List below.
Closely understanding interactions in a conversation, turn taking, use of pauses, nonverbal responses, and the influence these have on communication. **Your thoughts?**	Conversation analysis, where you can select small portions of interactional data that reflect detailed transcriptional notations, and analyze the small portions of data closely. Methodological approaches you could include but are not limited to: • Discourse analysis • Ethnomethodology • Actions implicative discourse analysis	
Artistic ways of thinking about your data inspired by poetry, dramas, theaters, documentaries, songs, fictions, nonfictions, satire, art, etc. **Your thoughts?**	Arts-based analysis where you would combine tenets of the genre of art you might be drawn to with the scholarly requirements of a study. You can conduct poetic analysis, dramatic analysis, visual analysis, etc. Often these approaches are not prescribed and it falls on the researcher to discover a process and document the process. Methodological approaches you could include but are not limited to: • Visual ethnography • Critical ethnography • Autoethnography • CRT and feminism methodologies • Case study • Narrative inquiry • Postmodern, poststructural, postcolonial methodologies	

What I am naturally drawn to is . . .	*You most probably will benefit from*	*Is there another approach that appeals to you? List below.*
Write what you might be drawn to that is not mentioned above.		

Representation of Your Work

Below are some possibilities of data representations. As you must have guessed by now, this list is not exhaustive and there are as many possibilities as there are qualitative researchers. Some of the references are dissertation works which will allow the readers to gain an in-depth understanding of the process that informed the decisions for the re-presentational format. If these dissertations are not available to you in electronic format, most libraries will be able to obtain them for you through interlibrary loan.

Thematic narratives—Often this is the format that most students are introduced to initially. This format follows an inductive analysis of data with the main themes being headings of the findings elaborated with various examples from the data. The narratives read like an explanation of theme in elaborate details. (See Bhattacharya, 2010; Jones, 2004.)

Phenomenological study—This kind of study usually has both theoretical and methodological influences of phenomenology. The structure of the representation is informed by the tenets of phenomenology. While there is wide variation in how people choose to understand and implement the tenets of phenomenology, there are some key aspects that tend to be common in these representations. These aspects focus on the structural analysis of the phenomenological experience in addition to the identification of essence. (See Bogard, 2011.)

Case study description—This kind of description is usually done through single or multiple case studies. Case studies can be both a methodological approach and/or representation. Often as a representation, scholars present the cases separately with thick, rich contextual details and then conduct a cross-case analysis if they have presented multiple cases. This allows the reader to understand each case within its individual context and gain an insight to how the authors compare and contrast their findings from the two cases. (See Bhattacharya, 2005; Clement, 2011; Stanley, 2013; Torres, 2012.)

Ethnographic description—This is a description of a culture that the researcher has studied. This description can take various forms as mentioned earlier. This description can be informed through interpretive, critical, and deconstructive perspectives. Additionally, there are also examples of visual ethnographies conducted using the tenets of ethnography and visual analysis. (See Geertz, 1973; Ladson-Billings, 2009; Lamb, 2000; Pink, 2001a; Visweswaran, 1994.)

Poetic re-presentation—These types of representation rely on creating poems based on the researcher's experience of data collection and analysis. There are many formats of doing so, and given that there are several ways in which one can construct a poem, researchers interested in this area are encouraged to study their chosen artistic genre carefully before integrating this representative approach in their research. (See Bhattacharya, 2007; Cahnmann, 2003.)

Narratives—Narratives can be formed through various analytic strategies. Often scholars who use narrative inquiry will also use narratives as representations. However, scholars who do not use narrative analysis specifically might still arrive at narratives as the form of representation through some analytic paths. It is important to remember that justification is always the key to how you are aligning different parts of the work to each other. (See Clandinin & Connelly, 2000; Kim, 2006.)

Ethnodrama—These types of representation usually involve some dramatic performance that demonstrates analyzing the data through some performative lens that allows creating plays. Usually ethnodramatic representations are written in the format of a play with dialogues, scene settings, and actions of the actors, as the researcher deems necessary. Various data sources inform the final dramatic rendering. (See Bhattacharya, 2009a; Gillen & Bhattacharya, 2013; Saldaña, 2005b.)

Other experimental/arts-based representations—There are enormous possibilities for arts-based and experimental representations. Sometimes people create a hybridized format of traditional and experimental representations and sometimes people explore with genres that are uncommon to the world of empirical research. If this is an area that appeals to you, then explore it broadly and deeply to fully internalize what it is that you like about this kind of representation and what theoretical and methodological work would need to be done for this work to meet academic rigor and be aesthetically aligned with the genre of your choice. (See Cahnmann-Taylor & Siegesmund, 2008; Sinner, Leggo, Irwin, Gouzouasis, & Grauer, 2006.)

Reflecting on Re-Presentations: Interactive Exercise

In this section, you will get a chance to document your thoughts, goals, and intentions about representing your research findings. Please note, as mentioned before, you will most likely return to this portion of the book repeatedly to sharpen your focus and understand how you situate yourself in relation to the study.

What would you like your representations of your findings to convey? What is important to you?

Which of the above types of representation appeals to you most? In what ways does it align with your intentions for representations? Are there other approaches that you might be interested in that are not documented here? What might they be and how do they align with your intentions?

Golden Nuggets: Summative Exercise

I offer you an infographic created by a former student, David Culkin, to organize everything we have spoken about in this book including the hourglass structure of research and various scholarly elements within a study. One infographic contains David's information, and there is a blank one for you to complete as you move through your study. This will appeal especially to visual learners.

David, a doctoral student in adult education, wanted to explore an autoethnographic study where he connected his experiences focusing on mental illness, death, and spirituality, and how such experiences speak to life span development of adults. He grounded his study in constructionism; his substantive framework was life events perspective. Methodologically he informed his study with autoethnography, situating autoethnography as a form of narrative inquiry of self in relation to certain cultural contexts. You will see these ideas and more represented in the hourglass model below.

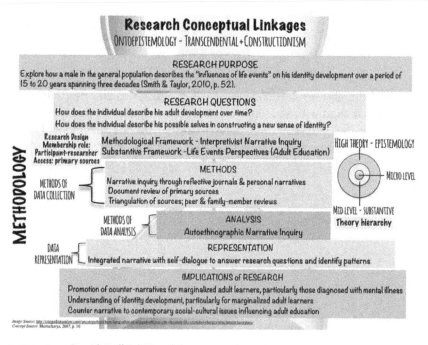

FIGURE 8.1   David Culkin's Visual Summary of His Dissertation Study

Complete the following infographic to organize your thoughts around your study.

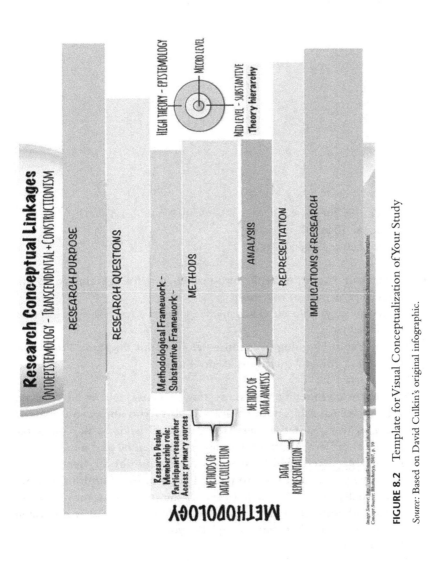

FIGURE 8.2 Template for Visual Conceptualization of Your Study

Source: Based on David Culkin's original infographic.

APPENDIX A

Wiki Project Interview of Doctoral Students, November 3, 2007
Interviewer: Kakali Bhattacharya
Participant: Carla (Pseudonym)

K: **Carla, again I want to thank you so much, um, for agreeing to do this interview as part of my study.**

C: Oh, you are quite welcome. It was an interesting experience being in that class, of course.

K: **Let me begin by going over some details about the study. Please feel free to ask me any questions at any time.**

C: Uh huh, okay.

K: **So we are conducting this study now because you and I have no grading relationship now. I want to talk to you about your experiences in my qualitative class when we used wikis to do collaborative class project. Anything you say is confidential and none of your identifying details will be shared with anyone for any reason. If at any time you do not want to participate, you can withdraw without any penalty. You will be able to see all the transcripts, make corrections, and consent to the findings before it is presented or published anywhere. Does that sound okay? Do you have any questions?**

C: No, it is pretty clear.

K: **Okay, wonderful. So let's start by maybe asking you about your first impression of wikis introduced in the class. Can you think of the first time wikis were introduced to class and what your experiences [were] of [them]?**

C: Well, as you know, um, I am a, um, a technophobe. I don't like technology and technology doesn't like me. I was worried. I already heard your class was hard and next thing you know, you are telling us about wakawaka wiki tiki stuff and I was like, what the hell? How am I expected to do this? This is not happening. My stress level was too high. And then you divided us into groups and so we had to work in groups. Group work is not the best thing for me. I don't always have good luck with it since people don't always put in equal efforts and some people end up carrying the rest. I hate group work. I really, really did not want to do the assignment. Plus, also I did not understand why we had to use wikis anyway. Why can't we do a group project and you post it on your website. I was really freaking out.

K: **That's really interesting to hear. So here you're freaking out about this assignment. But then you go look at what you say wakawaka wiki tiki.**

C: (laughs)

K: **Can you think of the first time when you used our wiki for the class project and tell me about it?**

C: Hmm. To tell you the truth, once I went to our class wiki page, I had no clue what I was looking at and what I was supposed to do. I just didn't. I was lucky I figured out how to just go to the class wiki page. That was already too much technology for me (laughs). And then I looked at the screen and I wondered, what on earth am I supposed to do with this? I just gave up. I walked away. I didn't want to do this. I just didn't. I called Sandy, one of my group members. He is a tech guru. I told him I am not getting this. So he told me to come by his office the next day. I went. And he showed me some stuff. And to tell you the truth, I still didn't know what on earth I was supposed to do. But it wasn't as bad as I thought. I think I made it too hard in my head. I told Sandy to just give me clear explicit directions when we do our project so that I can do what I was supposed to do. I was not happy, that's for sure.

K: **So Sandy became a peer mentor for you?**

C: Yes, he was. And every week we would work on the project together, he would talk to me after class, show me what I would need to do, and I would write it down, and he would do screenshots and send me those pictures via email. I would print them out and then have them on the side and then go through the task.

K: **Wow! That's quite elaborate. This was after I did the orientation in class for the wikis?**

C: Yes. Because the orientation was not helpful for me. My head wasn't in the game. I was lost. I didn't put the pieces of the puzzle together [until] much later. So you might as well have spoken Greek or done an interpretive dance. I wouldn't know one way or the other (laughs).

K: **How long did this continue on, where Sandy was making screenshots for you?**

C: Till the middle of the semester. Then the process became repetitive and then I wasn't so intimidated and I didn't say to myself that I couldn't do it because

I was doing it and I didn't break the computer, so it wasn't as bad as I thought it would be. But Sandy checked in on me after every class to make sure I was okay. That helped, knowing he was my security blanket. I would use the discussion thread to share my thoughts, reply back to my group people, and I would come back and check to see if my response was still there. And that was good. Sometimes I post things and it gets lost. Technology hates me. This was not the issue here. And I could track the history of who said what, so if I didn't understand something the first time around, I could come back and reread! That was really helpful.

APPENDIX B

Tuesday Night Trivia—Typical Day Vignette

It was another beautiful, breezy Tuesday night. I went to the local pub for the weekly trivia game. The sight inside the pub was typical of a Tuesday night. People were gathered around tables, talking, laughing, and sharing food and drinks. The music was somewhat loud, playing a country song. Looking over to my left by the window, I saw some of the members of the trivia team sitting at their usual table. Every Tuesday night, this pub hosts a trivia game. While some people are regular trivia players, others come and go as they please. The people I was observing were regular trivia attendants. It was now 9:00 p.m., and Adam, one of the early arrivers of the team, greeted me. There were some other early arrivers too, Art, Willy, and Chris. The players in this team are usually in their mid- to late twenties, either graduate students or working professionals. Between 9:00 and 9:15 p.m. most players arrived. Adam, the self-designated greeter, welcomed everyone and expressed his excitement over the pending game. The players who arrived were Brian, David, Sanjay, and Julia. The waitress, so familiar with this group, rarely asks what they want; instead she asks, "Are you going to have the usual?" As the group settled down in their seats, social conversations highlighting events of the past week, past performance in trivia, upcoming events flew across the table. A portion of the conversation would sound like:

SANJAY: I had a bad day today.
BRIAN: Why? What happened?
SANJAY: I got a bad grade in one of my essays and need to meet the professor.
BRIAN: Yes, go meet the professor.
ADAM: Hey, you guys, let's kick some butt this week.

CHRIS: Yeah, I am hungry and I want to win so that I don't have to pay for the food.

ADAM: Yes, and no more assumptions that women can't do the same thing as men. Shannon Doherty is just as good as Jason Priestly, people—we learnt from our last trivia. (Everyone laughs)

ART: If you guys want, we can go over to my place and play Balderdash after this.

CHRIS: That sounds like a good idea. Let's do it.

The conversation continued to flow until the announcer informed everyone that teams needed to submit their names. During my visit, this team had chosen one of the following names, Team X, Willfully Delusional, and SPIT (Special People in Trivia). Adam asked everyone about their preference for a name, and most people were happy with Willfully Delusional. Chris mentioned, "I am tired of Team X. Let's go with anything else, I don't care really." Willy echoed the same sentiment. Adam chose Willfully Delusional as the team name and submitted to the announcer. The game was then ready to begin.

It was 9:30 p.m. when the announcer began the game with the first question. Questions asked during trivia were of various types including world geography, U.S. presidents, movies, inventions, international politics, abbreviation, language, U.S. history, science, and music.

Generally, the questions have certain points assigned to them and the team can get those assigned points if they answered the question correctly. However, there are some questions that do have assigned points but have multiple answers as part of the complete correct answer. For example, "Who were the three singers for the soundtrack of *Three Musketeers*?" This question would require three correct answers from each team. The announcer informs that any incorrect answer would result in loss of points or negative scoring, unlike the other questions where incorrect answers did not result in loss of points, teams were just assigned a zero. If that was not complicated enough, to add more excitement and competitiveness, during each trivia game, teams are given three opportunities to bid points on certain questions before they know what the questions are. The announcer generally informs the category of the bid question, and the teams then decide how many points they would like to bid for that question. The announcer sets a maximum limit to the bidding. If the team answers a bid question correctly, then they would be awarded the number of bid points the team chose for themselves. If the team answers the question incorrectly, then the team would lose the exact number of points they bid from their current score. The bidding and the negative marking create decision-making opportunities, and it can be quite telling if someone's personal preference overrides the team's vote.

The first question asked was a question about music: "In what year was Guns N' Roses' *Appetite for Destruction* released?" Adam informed the group that he was pretty confident of Chris's knowledge on music and would defer it to Chris. Chris and Willy discussed to suggest an answer to the group.

CHRIS: It's either 1988 or 1987.

WILLY: Yeah, one of those two years.

CHRIS: If it was 1987, I would have heard of it, but since I don't remember and left the country in 1988, I must have missed it, so it has to be 1988.

WILLY: I still think it is 1987.

Julia joined in and agreed with Willy, "Yeah I think it's 1987 as well."

CHRIS: I don't think so, since I don't remember it releasing while I was in the country, it has to be when I left the country, which is 1988. So I would go with 1988.

Adam joined in and agreed with Chris.

ADAM: Yes, it has to be 1988, because I was in tenth grade then. So it's 1988, and that's the answer then.

Adam decided that it was 1988 and submitted the answer. To their surprise, the correct answer was 1987. Chris did not provide any further reasoning to accommodate the correct answer but mentioned to Julia, "You need to speak up more and sell your answers, so that we get them right for next time." Adam agreed and said, "Yes, people, you need to sell your answers to the rest of the team."

The questions continued. When it was time for a sports question, the team looked over at Willy and Brian. The question asked was, "Whose single-season strike-out record did Nolan Ryan break?" The team immediately referred the question to Willy and Brian, and they continued to deliberate on the answer. The following is an excerpt from Willy and Brian's deliberation:

BRIAN: I am writing Steve Carlton. Who else would you guess? The second all-timer, huh, may be Jim Palmer.

WILLY: No, not him, Jimmy Fox could be right.

BRIAN: Right, or maybe Bob Gibson.

WILLY: If you choose that, we would be going from positive to negative score. (Thinks for a while and exclaims) Hold on a second, who were the Jewish players?

BRIAN: (Laughs)

WILLY: I think it would be someone like Steve Carlton.

BRIAN: Yeah, but you have to remember who is number two.

WILLY: Okay, Steve Carlton it is.

To the surprise of Brian and Willy, they discovered that they were wrong. The answer was Sandy Kofex. Brian and Willy then discussed further to identify gaps in their thinking and rationalizing why Sandy Kofex would be the correct answer.

The team answered the rest of the questions correctly. The fact that Chris, Brian, or Willy provided incorrect answers did not compromise their roles as designated experts in music and sports, respectively. Adam designated himself as the expert in movies and answered a movie question without consulting others. The question was, "What Tom Hanks movie got an Oscar in 1996 and was nominated three times in a row?" Adam quickly wrote down *Apollo 13* as the answer and submitted it before showing it to others. He informed the team that he was very confident and did not need to consult. When the correct answer was announced, the team congratulated Adam on being right.

Apart from being right, Adam successfully convinced the team to bid conservatively when the announcer asked the team to bid. Since Adam likes to win, he hates being risky and taking chances, so he hardly ever votes for the maximum possible bid points unless the team is behind. When the announcer asked the teams to submit their bets (or bids), the team came to a decision-making point. The following is an excerpt from the conversation surrounding bidding:

The announcer asked, "Could you please hand in your bids for the next question? The category is geography and you can bid as much as 25 points."
Chris said, "Let's do it."
Art and Willy spoke simultaneously, "Yeah, let's do it."
David noted, "OK, we are doing it with 25 points," as he was writing down the bid points on the answer sheet.
Adam cautioned the team, "We are 17 points ahead. Should we consider bidding with lower points? We have been wrong today, you know, so it's better to be safe."
Willy mentioned, "I think we should just go for the whole 25 points."
Chris agreed with Willy and stated, "Let's go for it just for fun, come on."
Willy pushed the group, "Yeah, man, we are not playing lawyer trivia. We don't need to exercise caution. Let's have some fun."
Chris tells Adam, "You are too practical for your own good. Anyway, you are outvoted."
Adam retorted, "Listen, I am just asking for a compromise. Why can't we play for 20 points and not 25?"
David started to write down the points and said, "Then it is 20."
Willy disagreed. "Do the 25, man, I come here rarely, so I guess my opinion is one tenth of the entire group."
Adam put his foot down. "No, it's not like that. Everyone gets a vote just because they are here."
Sanjay suggested 20 points and Willy insisted on 25 again, while Chris asked, "What's the vote? Does it matter anyway? It's what Adam wants." David submitted 20 points for the bid question.
The question following the bidding was, "What country is bordered by the Red Sea and Persian Gulf?" When the music started, David turned to the group and said, "I know this one." He scribbled something on the answer sheet and

flashed it to the group. I saw that he had written down Saudi Arabia on the answer sheet. As David was showing the answer to the group, he repeated, "I know this, you guys can trust me on this one."

Chris raised some doubts and asked, "Does it border the Red Sea?"

Sanjay responded, "Yes, it does." Sanjay drew a map for Chris and showed the location of Saudi Arabia with respect to the Dead Sea and the Persian Gulf.

Art asked, "Are we sure?"

Sanjay reassured, "Yes, we are sure."

Chris pointed at Sanjay and said, "He said that it is OK to put down Saudi Arabia."

David submitted Saudi Arabia as the answer, and it was correct. As this was the last question, answering correctly put the team in first place and the team won. The players were ecstatic, they cheered and congratulated each other and eventually took their leave promising to hold their first place next week as well.

REFERENCES

Anzaldúa, G. (1999). *Borderlands la frontera: The new Mestiza*. San Francisco: Aunt Lute Books.

Banks, M. (2001). *Visual methods in social research*. London, UK: Sage Publications.

Barone, T., & Eisner, E.W. (2012). *Arts-based research*. Thousand Oaks, CA: Sage Publications.

Bateson, G., & Mead, M. (1942). *Balinese character*. New York, NY: New York Academy of Sciences.

Becker, H.S. (2002). Visual evidence: A seventh man, the specified generalization, and the work of the reader. *Visual Studies, 17*(1), 3–11.

Bhattacharya, K. (2005). *Border crossings and imagined nations: A case study of socio-cultural negotiations of two female Indian graduate students in the U.S.* Ph.D. Dissertation. University of Georgia. Athens, GA.

Bhattacharya, K. (2007). Voices lost and found: Using found poetry in qualitative research. In M. Cahnmann-Taylor & R. Siegesmund (Eds.), *Arts-based research in education: Foundations for practice* (pp. 83–88). New York, NY: Routledge.

Bhattacharya, K. (2009a). Negotiating shuttling between transnational experiences: A de/colonizing performance ethnography. *Qualitative Inquiry, 15*(6), 1061–1083.

Bhattacharya, K. (2009b). Othering research, researching the Other: De/colonizing approaches to qualitative inquiry. In J. Smart (Ed.), *Higher education: Handbook of theory and research* (Vol. XXIV, pp. 105–150). Dordrecht, The Netherlands: Springer.

Bhattacharya, K. (2010). Constructing democratic learning environments the wiki way. *Technology, Humanities, Narratives, and Education, Winter 2010*(8). Retrieved from http://thenjournal.org/index.php/then/article/view/48/47

Bhattacharya, K. (2013). A Second Life in qualitative research: Creating transformative experiences. In D.J. Loveless, B. Griffith, M.E. Bérci, E.T. Ortlieb, & P.M. Sullivan (Eds.), *Academic knowledge construction and multimodal curriculum development* (pp. 301–326). Hershey, PA: IGI Global.

Boellstorff, T., Nardi, B., Pearce, C., & Taylor, T.L. (2012). *Ethnography and virtual worlds: A handbook of method*. Princeton, NJ: Princeton University Press.

Bogard, G. (2011). *Un/masking domestic violence: A phenomenological exploration of mirrored transformative learning amongst instructors and batterers*. Dissertation. Texas A&M University–Corpus Christi. Corpus Christi, TX.

Bogdan, R.C., & Knopp Biklen, S. (2003). Data analysis and interpretation. *Qualitative research for education: An introduction to theory and methods* (4th ed.). Boston, New York, San Francisco: A & B.

Bromley, D.B. (1986). *The case-study method in psychology and related disciplines.* Chichester, UK: John Wiley & Sons.

Cahnmann, M. (2003). The craft, the practice, and possibility of poetry in educational research. *Educational Researcher, 32*(3), 29–36.

Cahnmann-Taylor, M. (2006). Reading, living, and writing bilingual poetry as SchoARTistry in the language arts classroom. *Language Arts, 83*(4), 342–352.

Cahnmann-Taylor, M., & Siegesmund, R. (2008). *Arts-based research in education: Foundations for practice.* New York, NY: Routledge.

Carspecken, P.F., & Apple, M. (1992). Critical qualitative research: Theory, methodology, and practice. In M.D. Lecompte & J. Preissle (Eds.), *The handbook of qualitative research in education.* San Diego, CA: Academic Press.

Charmaz, K. (2002). Qualitative interviewing and grounded theory analysis. In J. Gubrium & J.A. Holstein (Eds.), *Handbook of interview research* (pp. 675–694). Thousand Oaks, CA: Sage Publications.

Charmaz, K. (2006). *Constructing grounded theory: A practical guide through qualitative analysis.* Thousand Oaks, CA: Sage Publications.

Charmaz, K. (2008). Gathering rich data. *Constructing grounded theory: A practical guide through qualitative analysis* (pp. 13–41). Thousand Oaks, CA: Sage Publications.

Clandinin, D.J., & Connelly, F.M. (2000). *Narrative inquiry: Experience and story in qualitative research.* San Francisco, CA: Jossey-Bass.

Clement, S. (2011). *Friends and enemies in an inclusionary classroom: A comparative case study exploring transitional experiences of students with learning disabilities.* Dissertation. Texas A&M University–Corpus Christi. Corpus Christi, TX.

Clifford, J. (1994). Diasporas. *Cultural Anthropology, 9*, 302–338.

Cook, L. (2004). *Authoring self: Framing narratives of young women diagnosed with mood disorders.* Dissertation. University of Georgia. Athens, GA.

Crotty, M. (1998). *The foundations of social research: Meaning and perspective in the research process.* Thousand Oaks, CA: Sage Publications.

Delgado, R. (2000). *Critical race theory: The cutting edge* (2nd ed.). Philadelphia, PA: Temple University Press.

deMarrais, K. (2004). Qualitative interview studies: Learning through experience. In K. deMarrais & S.D. Lapan (Eds.), *Foundations for research: Methods of inquiry in education and the social sciences* (pp. 51–68). Mahwah, NJ: Lawrence Erlbaum Associates.

Denzin, N.K. (1989). *Interpretive biography.* Newbury Park, CA: Sage Publications.

Denzin, N.K., & Lincoln, Y.S. (Eds.). (2002). *The qualitative inquiry reader.* Thousand Oaks, CA: Sage Publications.

Denzin, N.K., & Lincoln, Y.S. (Eds.). (2005). *The Sage handbook of qualitative research.* Thousand Oaks, CA: Sage Publications.

Dewalt, K.M., & Dewalt, B.R. (2002). *Participant observation: A guide for fieldworkers.* Walnut Creek, CA: Altamira Press.

Dubois, W.E.B. (1899). *The Philadelphia negro: A social study.* Philadelphia, PA: University of Pennsylvania Press.

Ellis, C. (2008). *Revision: Autoethnographic reflections on life and work.* Walnut Creek, CA: Left Coast Press.

Engels, F. (1884/2010). *The origin of the family, private property and the state.* London, UK: Penguin Group.

Fine, M. (1991). *Framing dropouts: Notes on the politics of an urban public high school.* Albany, NY: State University of New York Press.

Foerstel, L., & Gilliam, A. (2009). *Confronting Margaret Mead: Scholarship, empire, and the South Pacific.* Philadelphia, PA: Temple University Press.

Gadamer, H.-G. (1989). *Truth and method.* New York, NY: Crossroad.

Gardner, P., & Cunningham, P. (1997). Oral history and teachers' professional practice: A wartime turning point? *Cambridge Journal of Education, 27*, 331–342.

Geertz, C. (1973). Deep play: Notes on the Balinese cockfight. *Daedalus,* Winter, 1–38.

Gillen, N.K., & Bhattacharya, K. (2013). Never a yellow bird, always a blue bird: Ethnodrama of a Latina learner's educational experiences in 1950–60s South Texas. *The Qualitative Report, 18*(Art. 28), 1–18.

Glaser, B.G. (1992). *Basics of grounded theory analysis: Emergence vs. forcing.* Mill Valley, CA: Sociology Press.

Glaser, B.G., & Strauss, A.L. (1967/2009). *The discovery of grounded theory: Strategies or qualitative research* (7th ed.). New Brunswick, NJ: Aldine Transaction.

Goodenough, W.H. (1973). *Culture, language, and society.* Reading, MA: Addison-Wesley.

Grewal, I., & Kaplan, C. (Eds.). (1994). *Postmodernity and transnational feminist practices.* Minneapolis, MN: University of Minnesota Press.

Hamel, J., Dufour, S., & Fortin, D. (1993). *Case study methods.* Newbury Park, CA: Sage Publications.

Heidegger, M. (1962). *Being and time.* Oxford, UK: Basil Blackwell.

Heidegger, M. (1982). *On the way to language.* New York, NY: Harper and Row Publishers.

Heron, J. (1967). *Feeling and personhood: Psychology in another key.* London, UK: Sage Publications.

Hine, C. (2000). *Virtual ethnography.* London, UK: Sage Publications.

hooks, b. (1990). *Ain't I a woman? Black women and feminism.* Boston, MA: South End Press.

Horst, H., & Miller, D. (Eds.). (2012). *Digital anthropology.* London, UK: Berg.

Hurston, Z.N. (1935). *Mules and men.* New York, NY: Negro University Press.

Husserl, E. (1931). *Ideas: General introduction to pure phenomenology.* London, UK: Allen & Unwin.

Jones, V. (2004). *Race is a verb: An effective history of young adults subjected to racial violence.* Dissertation. University of Georgia. Athens, GA.

Kaplan, C., & Grewal, I. (1999). Transnational feminist cultural studies: Beyond the Marxist/poststructuralism/feminism divides. In C. Kaplan, N. Alarcon, & M. Moallem (Eds.), *Between woman and nation: Nationalisms, transnational feminisms, and the state* (pp. 349–364). Durham, NC: Duke University Press.

Kim, J.H. (2006). For whom the school bell tolls: Conflicting voices inside an alternative high school. *International Journal of Education & the Arts, 7*(6), 1–22.

Knowles, J.G., & Cole, A.L. (2007). *Handbook of the arts in qualitative research: Perspectives, methodologies, examples, and issues.* Thousand Oaks, CA: Sage Publications.

Kvale, S., & Brinkmann, S. (2009). *InterViews: Learning the craft of qualitative research interviewing.* Thousand Oaks, CA: Sage Publications.

Ladson-Billings, G. (1998). Just what is critical race theory and what's it doing in a nice field like education? *Qualitative Studies in Education, 11*(1), 7–24.

Ladson-Billings, G. (2009). *The dreamkeepers: Successful teachers of African American children.* San Francisco, CA: Jossey-Bass.

Ladson-Billings, G., & Tate, W. (1995). Toward a critical race theory of education. *Teachers College Record, 97*(1), 47–67.

Lamb, S. (2000). *White saris and sweet mangoes*. Los Angeles, CA: University of California Press.

Lather, P. (1991). *Getting smart: Feminist research pedagogy with/in the postmodern*. New York, NY: Routledge.

Lather, P. (2006). Paradigm proliferation as a good thing to think with: Teaching research in education as a wild profusion. *International Journal of Qualitative Studies in Education, 19*(1), 35–57.

Lieblich, A., Tuval-Mashiach, R., & Zilber, T. (1998). *Narrative research: Reading, analysis, and interpretation*. Thousand Oaks, CA: Sage Publications.

Lincoln, Y.S., & Guba, E.G. (2002). Judging the quality of case study reports. In A.M. Huberman & M.B. Miles (Eds.), *The qualitative researcher's companion* (pp. 205–215). Thousand Oaks, CA: Sage Publications.

Madison, S.D. (2005). *Critical ethnography: Method, ethics, and performance*. Thousand Oaks, CA: Sage Publications.

Marton, F. (1986). Phenomenography: A research approach to investigating different understandings of reality. *Journal of Thought, 21*(3, Fall), 28–49.

Merleau-Ponty, M. (1962). *Phenomenology of perception* (C. Smith, trans.). London, UK: Routledge & Kegan Paul.

Merriam, S.B. (1998). *Qualitative research and case study applications in education*. San Francisco, CA: Jossey-Bass.

Mirzoeff, N. (Ed.) (2002/2012). *The visual culture reader* (2nd ed.). London, UK: Routledge.

Moustakas, C. (1994). *Phenomenological research methods*. Thousand Oaks, CA: Sage Publisher.

O'Brien, M. (2005). *John F. Kennedy*. New York, NY: Thomas Dunne Books.

Peshkin, A. (1988). In search of subjectivity—One's own. *Educational Researcher, 17*(7), 17–22.

Pink, S. (2001a). *Doing visual ethnography: Images, media and representation in research*. Thousand Oaks, CA: Sage Publications.

Pink, S. (2001b). Visual in ethnography: Photography, video, cultures and individuals. *Doing visual ethnography: Images, media and representation in research*. Thousand Oaks, CA: Sage Publications.

Polkinghorne, D.E. (1989). Phenomenological research methods. In R.S. Valle & S. Halling (Eds.), *Existential-phenomenological perspectives in psychology* (pp. 41–50). New York, NY: Plenum Press.

Preissle, J., & Grant, L. (2004). Fieldwork traditions: Ethnography and participant observations. In K. deMarrais & S.D. Lapan (Eds.), *Foundations for research: Methods of inquiry in education and the social sciences* (pp. 161–180). Mahwah, NJ: Lawrence Erlbaum Associates.

Richards, L. (2005). *Handling qualitative data: A practical guide*. Thousand Oaks, CA: Sage Publications.

Richardson, L. (2013). *After a fall: A sociomedical sojourn*. Walnut Creek, CA: Left Coast Press.

Ricoeur, P. (1967). *Husserl: An analysis of his phenomenology (Studies in phenomenology and existential philosophy)*. Evanston, IL: Northwestern University Press.

Ricoeur, P. (1976). *Interpretation theory: Discourse and surplus of meaning*. Fort Worth, TX: Texas Christian University Press.

Rolling, J.H. (2011). Cinderella story: An arts-based narrative research project. In N. Denzin & M. Giardina (Eds.), *Qualitative inquiry and global crises* (pp. 178–198). Walnut Creek, CA: Left Coast Press.

Rose, G. (2001/2012). *Visual methodologies: An introduction to the interpretation of visual materials*. London, UK: Sage Publications.

Ryan, G.W., & Bernard, H.R. (2003). Data management and analysis methods. In N.K. Denzin & Y.S. Lincoln (Eds.), *Collecting and interpreting qualitative materials* (2nd ed., pp. 259–309). Thousand Oaks, CA: Sage Publications.

Sadler, W.A. (1969). *Existence and love: A new approach in existential phenomenology.* New York, NY: Charles Scribner's Sons.

Saldaña, J. (2005a, January 7). *From page to stage: Autoethnography as monologue.* Paper presented at the 18th Annual Conference on Interdisiplinary Qualitative Studies. Athens, Georgia.

Saldaña, J. (Ed.) (2005b). *Ethnodrama: An anthology of reality theatre* (Vol. 5). Walnut Creek, CA: Altamira Press.

Schwandt, T.A. (2007). *The Sage dictionary of qualitative inquiry.* Thousand Oaks, CA: Sage Publications.

Sinner, A., Leggo, C., Irwin, R.L., Gouzouasis, P., & Grauer, K. (2006). Arts-based educational research dissertations: Reviewing the practices of new scholars. *Canadian Journal of Education, 29*(4), 1223–1270.

Smith, L.T. (1999/2012). *Decolonizing methodologies: Research and indigenous peoples* (2nd ed.). London, UK: Zed Books.

Spigelberg, H. (1982). *The phenomenological movement: A historical introduction* (3rd ed.). Boston, MA: Martinus Nijhoff.

Spradley, J.P. (1979). *The ethnographic interview.* Belmont, CA: Wadsworth Group.

St. Pierre, E.A. (1997). Methodology in the fold and the irruption of transgressive data. *International Journal of Qualitative Studies in Education, 10*(2), 175–189.

Stake, R. (1995). *The art of case study research.* Thousand Oaks, CA: Sage Publications.

Stanley, D. (2013). *Like a palm tree in a hurricane: A dual case study of digital text in the inclusive classroom.* Dissertation. Texas A&M University–Corpus Christi. Corpus Christi, TX.

Strauss, A., & Corbin, J.M. (1998). *Basics of qualitative research: Techniques and procedures for developing grounded theory* (2nd ed.). Thousand Oaks, CA: Sage Publications.

Strauss, A.L., & Corbin, J. (1998). *Basics of qualitaitve research: Techniques and procedures for developing grounded theory.* Thousand Oaks, CA: Sage Publications.

Torres, D. (2012). *The beady eye of professional development and appraisal system: A Foucauldian cross-case analysis of the teacher evaluation process.* Dissertation. Texas A&M University–Corpus Christi. Corpus Christi, TX.

Underberg, N.M., & Zorn, E. (2013). *Digital ethnography: Anthropology, narrative, and new media.* Austin, TX: University of Texas Press.

Upson, L. (2003). *Negotiating the mentor protégé relationship: What can be learned from the experience?* Dissertation. University of Georgia. Athens, GA.

Vagle, M.D., & Hofsess, B. (2016). Entangling a post-reflexivity through post-intentional phenomenology. *Qualitative Inquiry, 22*(5), 334–344.

van Maanen, J. (1988). *Tales of the field: On writing ethnography.* Chicago, IL: University of Chicago Press.

Visweswaran, K. (1994). *Fictions of feminist ethnography.* Minnesota, MN: University of Minnesota Press.

Wolcott, H.F. (1980). How to look like an anthropologist without being one. *Practicing Anthropology, 3*(2), 56–69.

Wolcott, H.F. (1992). Posturing in qualitative research. In M.D. LeCompte (Ed.), *The handbook of qualitative research in education* (pp. 3–52). San Diego, CA: Academic Press Inc.

Wolcott, H.F. (1995). *The art of fieldwork.* Walnut Creek, CA: AltaMira Press.

Wolf, M. (1992). *A thrice told tale: feminism, postmodernism, & ethnographic responsibility*. Stanford, CA: Stanford University Press.

Wolff, K.H. (1984). Surrender-and-catch and phenomenology. *Human Studies, 7*(2), 191–210.

Yin, R.K. (1994). *Case study research: Design and methods* (2nd ed.). Thousand Oaks, CA: Sage Publications.

Yin, R.K. (Ed.) (2003). *Case study research: Design and methods* (3rd ed.). Thousand Oaks, CA: Sage Publications.

INDEX

Page numbers in **bold** refer to tables. Page numbers in *italics* refer to figures.